THE
BLISS
OF
FREEDOM

A Contemporary Mystic's
Enlightening Journey

When the spirit within has found contentment, there radiates an aura that has an effect on all who are open to it. I have had the great privilege of experiencing this "effect" around Master Charles. He has a happiness that is contagious, and leaves the soul feeling joyful. Knowing him is a journey that has unlimited potential, and allows us to be more independent, healthy, and happy. A true gift in a troubled world.

—*Cherie de Haas, Naturopath, Author, and Television Presenter, Melbourne, Australia*

The human being is a vast organic system, open to the world and dependent upon its influences. All healing begins with this holistic truth, embracing the oneness of humanity, society, and nature. Only this approach heals the spirit and emotions as well as the body. Master Charles embodies this holistic reverence for the light of life, inspiring us through his own life of light.

—*Dr. James Ye Xu, Heart Surgeon and Chinese Medical Practitioner, Melbourne, Australia*

It is difficult to verbalize an experience of the heart. . . . Master Charles lives his truth, which obliges us to look at our own truth.

—*Ben Olstein, D.D.S., Caulfield, Australia*

Master Charles has been an inspiration. He has taught me much about meditation, awareness, and consciousness, and my spiritual practice has grown and matured through his influence. Whenever I am with him, I experience a contagious, expansive, sublime energy.

—*Michael Horwitz, M.D., Grand Junction, Colorado*

Thanks to Master Charles, happiness, peace, and freedom have come back into my life.

—*Enrique Molina, Corporate Vice-President, Mexico City*

Master Charles is a true embodiment of the celebration of life.

—*Rick Pallack, Men's Wear Designer, Sherman Oaks, California*

The Bliss of Freedom is the description in contemporary words of a time-honored relationship of the master and disciple, and the powerful experiences which happen after initiation.

—*Mahamandaleshwar Swami Nityananda,*
Haridwar, India/Pine Bush, New York

My first encounter with Master Charles was the beginning of the most exciting, intense, indescribable period of my life. During the ensuing years of association, I have had profound mystical experiences, gained a clarity I never believed possible, and cleared away many of the limiting concepts and conditionings of my fundamentalist childhood. It is very freeing!

—*Paul Shannon, Physicist, Washington, D.C.*

Master Charles offers the greatest challenge in life—true awareness. His life not only demonstrates that it is possible, but shows us moment to moment the outcome—true freedom.

—*Kip Mazuy, Musician, Bessington, Vermont*

Like the archetypal hero, Master Charles has encountered the depths and heights of his own being. He has returned from the journey a true master, whose expanded presence is a catalyst for those lucky enough to meditate with him.

—*Marita Digney, Jungian Analyst,*
Philadelphia, Pennsylvania

To describe Master Charles in words does not do him justice. The person and the energetic presence have to be experienced. A few moments with this enlightening master can open windows to the soul.

—*Sharon Haase, Occupational Therapist,*
Newfoundland, Canada

Prior to meeting Master Charles, I had only read, with envy and amazement, about the mystical experience. Being with Master Charles brought it within my reach.

—*David Downey, M.D., Auckland, New Zealand*

As a radical, retired Anglican priest, I consider Master Charles to be the most Christlike man I have ever met. He has the amazing ability to put his finger on parts of me that I would rather not know about. In doing so, he lures me gently and lovingly towards my own center.

—*Jeremy Shaw, Anglican Priest, Auckland, New Zealand*

With humor and bliss, Master Charles holds open the portal of the soul. It is there that one finds God as the splendor of one's own true selfless self. This is the breathless wonder of liberation!

—*F. Pearl McBroom, M.D.,*
Pacific Palisades Highlands, California

When I met Master Charles, the truth of my own being was revealed. An experience I had longed for so much, read about, contemplated—yet never believed that I ever would be able to attain. The ability to give us a glimpse of our true nature is the "proof" of a true mystic. Master Charles is without any doubt one of the very few living mystics of our times.

—*Marlena Simon, Aschaffenburg, Germany*

Association with a contemporary mystic such as Master Charles is a rare privilege. I revel in the mysteriously penetrating, yet warmly comforting, joy I feel in his presence, and the sense of infinite wonder in my own power revealed. He shows me the only true freedom I have ever known.

—*Phil Justice, Engineer, Greensboro, North Carolina*

Meeting Master Charles started me on a journey of challenging my beliefs and the validity of all my accumulated "knowledge." Many of my concepts have been shattered, but have been replaced by the experience of greater clarity and calmness in all areas of my life. Master Charles is an inspiration to explore mysticism, not philosophically, but rather experientially and to move beyond what I know.

—*Rudolf A. Kaufmann, Psychotherapist and*
Management Consultant, Bremen, Germany

Synchronicity programs and retreats with Master Charles are a journey of the deepest dimension of love—self-love . . . a must for any spiritual seeker of truth in these times.

—*Joel Holt, B.A., Jewelry Artist, Dallas, Texas*

Since meeting Master Charles, and becoming a regular meditator, the things that I liked least about myself—poses and disguises, costumes of the soul—have slipped away. Greater illumination takes their place. My world is more peaceful now than it has ever been.

—*Joan Alk, Registered Nurse, Port Townsend, Washington*

I am as skeptical as they come, but there is no ignoring someone like Master Charles! He exudes an energy presence that is addictively palpable. I can *feel* change happening within me. My body tingles and relaxes; my mind slows down and stress disappears. This happens whenever I am close to him. He doesn't have to say a thing; it is just the way he is.

—*Al Stacey, Helicopter Pilot, Kamloops, B.C., Canada*

In Homer's Odyssey, Odysseus took delight in a certain man because he knew how to give good welcome. Like that man, Master Charles has the same quality to give good welcome to many.

—*Stephen Feinberg, Chairman, St. John's University,*
Annapolis/Santa Fe

It appears that now, for the first time in history, we have someone who has learned from the masters of the Far East and has brought this wisdom to the West through his book, *The Bliss of Freedom.* I am looking forward to learning his new technique of meditation, as I feel this is the missing link in my being able to find the true source of life in this form. Thanks to this book, I feel as if I have truly met a master of the Far East.

—*William Turner, Founder of the Wisdom Network*
and Turner Vision

THE BLISS OF FREEDOM

*A Contemporary Mystic's
Enlightening Journey*

MASTER CHARLES

ACACIA
PUBLISHING
CORPORATION

Published by Acacia Publishing Corporation
23852 Pacific Coast Highway, Suite 756
Malibu, CA 90265

Editor: Nancy Grimley Carleton
Editorial Assistant: Claudette Charbonneau
Cover Art: "The Creation Game" by Suesy Circosta
Cover Design: Lightbourne Images
Back Cover Photo: Photoworks of Virginia
Book Design and Composition: Classic Typography

Manufactured in the United States of America.

10 9 8 7 6 5 4 3 2 1

Library of Congress Cataloging-in-Publication Data
Charles, Master.
    The bliss of freedom : a contemporary mystic's enlightening
journey / Master Charles.
        p. cm.
    ISBN 0–9650958–2–7 (pbk.)
    1. Charles, Master.   2. Spiritual biography—United States.
I. Title.
BL73.C38A3   1996
291.4'092—dc20
    [B]   96–36541
                                                          CIP

Dedication

To the unity of diversity

Acacia publishes books that inspire personal growth and health in heart, mind, body, and spirit, and raise people's consciousness to align with nature and promote planetary healing and balance.

Contents

    An unnumbered photo section
    appears following page 236.

Foreword

In some ways, I'm the last person you would expect to be writing the Foreword to a book by an enlightening mystic and master of meditation. Before 1991, my life was that of a modern-day "pirate": private jets, multimillion-dollar take-overs, gambling casinos, a movie company, a savings and loan, and even a position in the Nixon administration. Despite my worldly success, however, my daily experience was one of fear, anxiety, hate, and constant misery and self-loathing. At that time, the closest thing I had to a mantra was the saying "Life is a bitch, and then you die."

I met Master Charles by accident in July 1991. In an attempt to escape the stress of a pending federal lawsuit, I attended a weeklong Synchronicity Conscious Living and Contemporary Meditation retreat with a friend and business associate. I felt an initial repulsion toward Master Charles the first day of the retreat. The second day of the program, I asked him why I found him, his voice, and even his picture so hateful. By the seventh day, much to my shock and amazement, I blurted out my unconditional love for him.

How did this change happen? Simple. I experienced a truly enlightening human being. Master Charles's unconditional love and acceptance, once I became open to it, changed my life at its very core. On the surface, I remain a "pirate," but by many miracles or one miracle, my inner experience has changed radically. I have now learned to love and accept myself, my life, and everything in it, which, interestingly enough, still includes jets, yachts, and business deals, as well as anxiety, sadness, and the full range of human emotions. But now I experience all of this as a glorious celebration. More and more, I live my life as a dream movie "for the fun of it," my mantra simply being "It's all just a movie—so what!"

So read this book, and discover for yourself the unique human being that is Master Charles. Then relax and enjoy your own movie—as saint, pirate, or whatever role you choose. It feels the same to me these days.

Michael Lang
Chairman
Synchronicity Foundation, Virginia

Preface

At one time or another, we have all heard the saying "When the student is ready, the teacher appears." This simple adage has been applied to almost every learning situation that a human being encounters in life. In the most ancient of spiritual traditions, however, it refers specifically to the advent of the enlightening mystical master into one's life, and the transformational journey that then unfolds.

The initial experience of the encounter between master and disciple is marked by the transmission of a profound awakening, a radical expansion of awareness accompanied by the truthful mystical insight that unmistakably demonstrates the authenticity of the enlightening master. This transmission of energy moves the student beyond the familiar boundaries of the mind and into the multifaceted dimensions of an eternal reality of oneness—a cosmic unity in diversity. Thereafter, the student continues the spiritual journey under the mystical master's guidance and within the environment of his enlightening energy field. Just as modern science speaks of the process of entrainment, wherein, according to the principles of sound, the lower frequency sound can pull others toward its slower vibration and greater amplitude, so the energy field of the enlightening master entrains or empowers that of the student, until ultimately the experience of an enlightening state of being, an unending awareness of God, or Source, becomes constant.

In the purest of contexts, this is a natural and spontaneous process. It is analogous to the process of absorbing sunlight. If you want to experience light, simply place yourself within proximity of the sun, and illumination is inevitable. If you want to get a suntan, expose yourself daily to the sun. If you want to experience the ultimate truth, place yourself within relationship to one who is already anchored in this truth, and inevitably you will learn from the master's authentic example. This time-honored mystical tradition transcends any one religious path and is known as the master-disciple relationship. The result is no less than absolute freedom.

In my life, I have been blessed to have had an enlightening master who empowered me as I opened to a constant awareness of the truth of the oneness of all that is. In this book, within the limitations of words, I attempt to express the heart of this enlightening experience, through reflection on the major themes of Source, Mastership, Surrender, Love, and Freedom.

My own journey, like everyone's, has been unique in its unfolding. From the pool of infinite possibilities, I have explored the mystical path, and my experience continues with all its magic and miracle even in this moment. It is a blissful moment, filled with the liberating awareness of the oneness of all that is. It is this truthful awareness, the awareness of our oneness, that I joyfully share with you

now. Come, look through my eyes. Live through my being.
Share with me the bliss of freedom.

Master Charles
Spring 1996
Synchronicity Foundation, Virginia

Acknowledgments

I want to gratefully acknowledge the many individuals who helped make this book possible, and rather than name each one of them, I offer this heartfelt tribute of gratitude:

To the diversity of unity

Master Charles
Synchronicity Foundation, Virginia

INTRODUCTION

Awakening . . .
Flame ignites flame
Light bursts into light
Darkness disappears
The veil is lifted
One luminous consciousness reveals itself
To itself, for the sake of itself
Existence . . . awareness . . . bliss
An eternally delighting reality
I am
All is
Source

CHAPTER 1

Awakenings

Each moment contains a hundred messages from God.
To every cry of "Oh Lord," God answers a hundred times,
"I am here."

RUMI

It was an early spring day in 1970, shortly before my twenty-fifth birthday, and I was visiting friends who had just returned from a business trip to India and other Far Eastern countries. While sharing their travels with me, they talked about having met an enlightened master in India. They seemed most devout as they described the encounter, for he had impressed them with his illumination, and they had experienced deep spiritual inspiration.

They asked if I would like to see a photograph of him. When I agreed, they handed me a small card designed like a temple with folding flaps for doors. I opened it casually and looked at the black-and-white photograph of the man inside. If I had a million words, I could not adequately describe the magnitude of what I experienced over the next few hours.

As I focused on the photograph, my eyes seemed to lock in an open gaze, and my whole body followed, relinquishing all volitional control. The photograph dissolved into a whirlpool of scintillating, hallucinogenic energy. I was immersed in a rose- and blue-colored magnificence, permeated with minute particles of dancing, diamondlike light that slowly moved upward and entered the area just above the center of my eyebrows.

A multitudinous explosion erupted from the depths of my being and reverberated through every dimension of my perception, as an intoxicating bliss saturated me from head to toe. The most sacred peace filled all and everything. Time was suspended within an all-encompassing stillness, and from the subtlest dimensions an ethereal and heavenly music softly echoed—violins, harps, a lone flute, and the tinkling of a thousand glass wind chimes sounding within the harmonic oneness of an angelic choir.

I experienced a divine, awe-inspiring, yet totally nurturing contentment beyond all contentment. Wave upon wave of undulating ecstasy radiated outward to infinity. Everything within this shimmering reverberation was disappearing and reappearing, all form dissolving into itself, a reflection of hallucinogenic light within an ocean of delight.

I continued to observe my two friends, but their bodies had become multidimensional. I could see to the utmost core of their beings, which in each case was a small point of iridescent blue light. Luminosity flowed in all directions from these points of blue light, manifesting as their forms and intermingling with all other forms as they blended one into the other.

All and everything manifested as a merging sea of blissful, luminous energy, joyously delighting within itself— the most beautiful reality that one could ever imagine. This was divine existence, absolute, free, and independent, celebrating itself for the sake of itself. This was the one without a second, a pure awareness through which an otherworldly voice reverberated its truth: "I am one. . . . I am free. . . . I am all that is."

Suspended within this awareness beyond all time, I merged in it, flowing, floating, dancing, delighting, enjoying the freedom of oneness as I remained a quiescent witness. My mind was stilled in awe of the heavenly majesty. Bliss consumed every cell of my being. The loving voice again reiterated its affirmation: "I am one. . . . I am free. . . . I am the play of consciousness. . . . I am all that is. . . . I am. . . . I . . . I . . . I . . ." The ethereal echo gradually disappeared as it was reabsorbed into the fullness of its all-pervasive unity.

I remained within the ecstasy of this incredible reality for what seemed like an eternity, and then ever so gently it diminished, contracting itself and condensing into physicality. The energy released itself through the space between my eyebrows, and like a whirlpool wound its way back into the photograph in my hands.

My body unlocked, along with my gaze, and everything seemed to return to normal, yet I was never to be the same. For I had come face to face with the divine. I had scaled the heights of the ultimate reality that I considered to be God alone, Source alone, and nothing else could ever take its place.

As I went through this mystical experience, my friends were very supportive and understanding. They honored what was happening, and from their time in India they knew enough to be still and watch. Three hours had passed from the time they presented me with the photograph. My friends acknowledged the profundity of what had just transpired and said that obviously I had a special connection with the man whose photograph had catalyzed the experience. They added that they thought I would meet him soon, and that a great journey was about to begin in my life.

I nodded my agreement, and then I asked them who this man was, for they had neglected to mention his name. They both smiled and said, "His name is Muktananda. It means 'the bliss of freedom.'"

Alone after my friends had left, I sat quietly, contemplating the experience. My entire world had changed, and I felt completely different, for mystical awareness continued its subtle reverberation within me, and a palpable peace saturated the whole of my being. As I considered how I had arrived at these precious moments, key incidents in my life flashed before me, and the mysterious pieces fell together like pieces in a kaleidoscope, leading me to a deeper understanding of my life than I had ever had before. I had been told many times that one day I would understand, and now it was happening. The whole of my life, up to that moment, seemed ever so appropriate.

I was born on March 14, 1945, at about ten o'clock in the morning. It was a snowy winter day in Syracuse, New York. My parents were a loving couple of Italian-American descent. They had been married several years, and I was their second child, following my sister, who was three years older. Their third child, my younger sister, would be born some years later, when I was fourteen. Throughout my early childhood years, my parents nurtured me with all the love and care and security that bring any child to an appropriate flowering in time.

My first constant stream of awareness manifested at about three years of age. I observed myself sitting out in front of our house on the sewer vent, which was shaped like a mushroom and just the right size to serve as a perfect seat from which to observe the world and all its happenings. People passed by and occasionally stopped to chat, but I was immersed in my play, focused on a sea of toys and imaginary fantasies. My childhood was truly glorious, filled with all the typical middle-class American accoutrements. We delighted in baby ducks at Easter, Santa Claus at Christmastime, and all manner of joyful family experiences. After dinner during the summertime, we would all pile into the family car, and Dad would drive us to the ice cream shop for a special treat.

I remember magical days of shopping with my mother, the highlight of which was a visit to Woolworth's, where I had the opportunity to pick out a small toy for myself. We played in the snow in the winter and went swimming and on picnics in the summer. We had many friends and relatives, and we drove to the bakery each afternoon to get hot, freshly baked Italian bread for dinner. We would invariably eat half a loaf on the way home in the car. I can still taste the warm and fragrant magnificence of the bread on the cold and wintry days of my memory. My delightful childhood continued in this way with one minor disturbance.

My body was somehow extremely sensitive to the surrounding environment, and I was plagued with every allergy known in those times. My skin was covered with rashes, and the constant itching was truly horrible. At night I had to sleep with gloves on my hands to keep me from tearing my flesh from the bones with my constant scratching. I vividly remember the gloves because a hole had to be cut out so that I could suck my left thumb without interference. Sucking my thumb was my lone soothing comfort during those long nights of suffering.

I endured constant medical testing and treatment, including multiple medicines, special diets, and every conceivable manner of environmental restriction: no pets, no dust, no feathers, and no friends, most of whom had abandoned me because their mothers were afraid I had some contagious disease. When all the medicines, pills, and salves proved ineffective, my doctors suggested that the family relocate to a different climate in the hope that this would assist in my healing. I was about eight years old at the time.

Appropriately enough, we had close relatives in southern Florida, and since my father also suffered from allergies, we eventually relocated there. Over the course of a few years, and with the advent of puberty, my physical ailments gradually subsided, and all the scars vanished. I adjusted and made new friends, and life went on.

From a young age, I was filled with a deep spiritual longing. As my family was of Italian-American heritage, I was raised in the Roman Catholic religion. I received a Catholic education through high school, and I was as thoroughly indoctrinated as anyone who is ever involved in an organized religion. Up until the age of ten, I did not show much interest in Catholicism, and I felt somewhat rebellious toward the church and all its dogmas. On Sundays I would rather have stayed home and played with my toys than gone to mass. When my parents dragged me along anyway, they invariably ended up scolding me for my misbehavior as we drove home. Perhaps this served as an omen of the future, when I would renounce Catholicism completely.

But even while I was resisting going to Sunday mass, I managed to find an affinity with God within the Catholic context. I became identified with the Virgin Mother of Christ as my chosen manifestation of deity. The Virgin Mother was the first form of God as Mother that I recognized, and toward which I was drawn irresistibly. Somehow, I experienced a connection with her that went beyond my comprehension, yet mysteriously I did not need to understand. This connection felt old and familiar, yet simultaneously new and unknown.

The first altar I ever made I dedicated to the Virgin Mother as a representation of Godliness. The theme of God as Mother has inspired me ever since. I understand it more now than I did then, but the experience has always been overwhelming and awe inspiring, and continues to be so, even as I write this.

The first experience I recall of God as Mother happened when I was about four years old. At night, as I was drifting off to sleep, I would hear a beautiful voice softly calling my name within the enveloping darkness of the room. This sound did not frighten me, because it was accompanied by a peaceful presence that simultaneously filled the space. As the gentle calling continued, refractions of light would illuminate the blackness, and the whole room would dance with vibrating energy. I experienced this as a kind of sacred celebration. The voice sounded motherly, loving, and nurturing, and within this entrancing manifestation, I would eventually fall asleep.

I heard this voice on a regular basis throughout my early childhood. Sometimes it was accompanied by very subtle celestial music—harps, flutes, tinkling glass wind chimes, and an ethereal harmonic choir. It was like a mother's loving lullaby, soothing her child into the peaceful bliss of a deeply nurturing sleep.

After a year or two of this calling, I began to see a form emerging within the light at the end of my bed. The form manifested as pure luminescence radiating from its center-most point, each particle of light a delight in slow motion. I identified the form as that of the Virgin Mother, since that was the only mental interpretation I could come up with based on my Catholic background. It was the Virgin Mother, yet somehow different. The robes were similar, and the head hooded, but the arms and hands were thrown over the head in a posture of absolute abandon to ecstasy. This magnificent apparition expressed a sublime celebration, as if the whole of creation was an extension of its form.

As this Godly Mother called to me, I would drift into sleep, entranced by her divinely intoxicating love. Visionary dreams permeated my sleep throughout these years, all involving this form of God as Mother. She would appear in all manner of situations, and we would play together as mother and child. I experienced this as sacred and sublime, yet also as normal and delightful. A deep trust evolved between us, and through this trust we formed a bond that allowed me an ever-expanding experience.

As I awakened one morning at about the age of nine, I became aware of an intoxicating sensation of peace and love saturating my body. The whole room shimmered with the intensity of the brightest light dancing across the ripples of a pond, and infinitesimal particles of luminosity reflected light one unto another. I was lying in bed on my back, and my body suddenly locked in this position. My awareness skyrocketed upward, as everything within me seemed to move heavenward at an incredible velocity.

Then all volitional control over my mind vanished. For a moment, fear stroked my heart as I relinquished the safe and familiar boundaries to which I was accustomed. It was no longer possible to be anything but a witness to what was happening, as my mind began to repeat over and over: "I am. . . . I am. . . . I am. . . ." Then, as my awareness swiftly ascended and expanded, it added: "I am God. . . . I am God. . . . I am God." I watched as the repetition continued until my awareness again exploded, and I ascended beyond the mind, leaving it and the repeating words in the lower distance.

Everything became increasingly more subtle until all form disappeared. All that remained was pure awareness, a conscious identification with God and as God, both with form and without form. Then all form vanished, and I, as pure awareness, remained merged in the silent, blissful stillness of oceanic oneness, forever beyond all and everything.

After an hour within this state of absorption, I descended in reverse progression, through the nonvolitional mind with its repetition of the words "I am God," into the volitional mind and the re-creation of safe boundaries, through the release of the body lock, and once again into the rapture of the moment in that bed and that room. I was totally saturated with peace and bliss. Not wanting to move, I lay there for some time recalling what had just happened and reveling in the rapturous experience I was still enjoying. All fear had vanished, for my mind was absolutely still. I was consumed in the experience of truthful oneness. Slowly, ever so gently, I returned to normal consciousness.

I contemplated this experience for a long time, just as I had found myself contemplating many of my earlier moments of bliss. I had discovered early on that no one else I knew shared such experiences. Therefore, I constantly searched for answers and tried to find some frame of reference for what was happening in my ever-so-secret world.

My parents could not answer my questions in this regard, nor could my teachers, religious and otherwise. Eventually I stopped asking, while never ceasing the search for understanding. My life became a quest of trying to comprehend what I was experiencing, what it meant, and why it was happening to me. I continued this search for many years.

Just as some people show a strong ambition even as young children to pursue careers as musicians or scientists, writers or entrepreneurs, so I at an early age longed for answers to my spiritual questions. Those who find particular success in their chosen fields of endeavor are generally those who are best able to maintain a focused, one-pointed attention on their goal. Just as J. P. Morgan focused from an early age on the accumulation of capital, or Vincent van Gogh immersed himself in his art, so I focused on the blissful mystical moments I had experienced since early childhood.

What fascinated me most in all these experiences through the years of my youth was the state of pure freedom I enjoyed when they happened. It seemed as though I transcended all boundaries and became unlimited, absolutely free, like an eagle soaring on the wind, flowing and floating without any effort whatsoever. This was total freedom, a blissful ecstasy that was eternally clear and pure. While within it, I was fulfilled. Without it, I longed for it alone. I knew it was Godly. I knew it was all I wanted or needed, and I continued to seek it, consumed with its exploration as the days passed into years, and the perfection of the journey unfolded.

From my earliest years, it became apparent that my destiny would involve the greater public. My maternal grandmother had a great fondness for the world of entertainment. She had wanted to be a performer herself but had not fulfilled the desire. She therefore sowed the seed of this dream in her grandchildren. Of all of them, I was the one in which it flowered. Along the way, I received music lessons, as well as dancing, singing, and acting lessons, and by the ripe old age of five, I was modeling children's clothing. As the years progressed, I regularly appeared in public presentations, and through my most formative years, I was often onstage in front of an audience. I became quite comfortable with a public life.

By the time I was a teenager, I had an acknowledged stage presence that seemed like second nature. It was easy for me to appear before an audience, and large numbers of people never frightened me at all. In the years to come, the creative talents my grandmother had nurtured would find their true expression, but in those days of my adolescence I simply enjoyed it all, simultaneously wondering why it was happening, and why it was necessary. For the spiritual dimensions of my life also continued without interruption.

Throughout my teens, not only did I enjoy regular mystical experiences in the sanctity of my private world, I also experienced them during my public presentations. In the middle of a stage performance, the most incredible Godly manifestations would emerge to surprise me. I remember one of these experiences with particular amusement.

I was about fourteen at the time, and by a series of coincidences I was touring with a carnival burlesque show during my summer vacation from school. I played the drums for the exotic dancers, as they were called professionally. One night in the middle of the show, my awareness suddenly expanded, and I entered into the state of witness consciousness that up to that point I had only experienced in the privacy of my own home. I could observe my body playing the drums and my eyes watching the movements of the dancers, yet my awareness included very subtle dimensions. Everything was bathed in indigo blue light. In the middle of this holographic scene, she appeared—the one I identified as God the Mother and had experienced so often during my sleep time. Now she was here in my waking moment, and she began to dance to the beat of my drums, while slowly merging with all the dancers. Through them, within them, dancing all around them and dissolving all boundaries, she danced ecstatically, and her dance was much more exotic than that of the other dancers.

She was truly celebrating, dancing with an absolute absorption in the moment, for it was her all-consuming, divine dance, the universal dance of all creation. I was intoxicated with the bliss of her presence, and everything was bathed in her luminous radiance. It seemed as though the dance lasted forever, yet it was no longer than the usual performance, and by the conclusion I had slowly returned to my normal waking perception. I remained expanded in awareness, and I could hear her voice calling in the distant recesses of my being: "I am God. . . . I am God. . . . I am the eternal dance of one consciousness. . . . I am the dance of life itself. . . . I am all that is. . . ."

I was overwhelmed by such manifestations, and I continued to contemplate their meaning and message. The message concerned the oneness of all existence, and also demanded that I bring together the subjective and objective polarities of my world. God was both unity and diversity, and also beyond. These experiences filled me with awe. I only wanted more, and the quest for this totally consumed my mind.

I sometimes wondered why I was involved in the public life of the entertainment world. Whenever I asked this question within myself, I was simply made aware that it was all preparation, and that I would understand one day.

I was meant to learn from all that presented itself in my world and not worry about why it was happening or what it meant. I simply needed to trust, and to experience all that came my way.

At the same time I was involved in the entertainment world, I was also managing to enjoy some aspects of the Catholic experience through my studies at a Catholic high school. Daily exposure to the nuns and priests, who taught us the principles and history of Catholicism, sparked my interest in the religious vocation I heard described in my daily religion classes.

At times as I neared the end of high school, I even considered joining a religious order, becoming a monk, and withdrawing from the world to the quiet solitude of a mystical life. I was encouraged in this by the nuns and priests who taught me in the Catholic schools I attended. But the Catholic religious context seemed too limited, so I continued my involvement in the magical world of entertainment and academic education, also enjoying such typical teenage pursuits as playing football, being an honors student, and attending the prom, wondering where it would all lead. Above all, I trusted the divine guidance of God as Mother, for she was more real to me than anything else I experienced.

During the days of my youth, I sought guidance from certain of my teachers. Each one taught me many things and added to my discipline and focus. I grew in my ability to remain one-pointed in all that I did. Yet my earthly teachers could not answer my mystical questions, for the mystical realm lay beyond the scope of their experience. My deeper adventure continued without any spiritual guidance save that which the Divine Mother brought to me.

Because of all the time I spent in the world of entertainment, I became fascinated with the creative process. In moments of focus as a performer, I experienced considerable expansions of awareness. I observed the connection between the focusing of the mind and the awareness that accompanied it. It seemed as if the mind stopped, and in its suspension the creative experience expressed itself. The creative process was powerful and fulfilling, though not as blissfully profound as the mystical experiences that I continued to enjoy. The connection between the two intrigued me, and I intuitively knew that they were related. I continually studied this connection and questioned all the performers I knew about their experience. It was not until many years thereafter that I fully understood.

Creative inspiration is simply a natural expression of God, of Source, and it always flows through a quiet mind. The more focused, the more meditative, and the more aware of Source one is, the more creative one is. When we access the field of truthful reality, we are creative. These were the constant meditations of my youth, the journey of the creative artist I was at the time. Meditation assumes many forms, and this was a dominant one in my progressive unfolding. Without knowing it, I was meditating every day, privately and publicly, subjectively and objectively, and my awareness was forever expanding.

As my teenage years progressed, I began to move beyond the limited boundaries of organized religion. I could see the fraud and hypocrisy in those who presented religion to me, and I could not relate my regularly occurring mystical experiences to the religion I heard preached within the confines of the church. In my search for answers and a greater understanding of my spiritual experiences, I began to explore many new and different spiritual traditions.

As I left my teenage years behind me and moved out on my own, I practiced Zen Buddhism for a while, for it seemed to relate most directly to my own perceived reality. I adopted a lifestyle of simplicity. When I was living on my own in an apartment, a friend who lived downstairs came up with a bowl of brown rice one evening, and I was inspired to read a book on macrobiotics. I became a vegetarian and celebrated my joyful serenity all the more.

As I moved beyond the limited boundaries of religion, I began to explore metaphysical traditions, seeking answers to the questions that conventional religion did not address. I learned astrology, which I had known intuitively even as a teenager. I studied psychic phenomena such as ESP, astral projection, and awareness expansion through biofeedback. All of these explorations broadened my horizons and opened me to a world of incredible diversity. Although I came closer to understanding my own mystical experiences, somehow I always fell just a little short. I longed to find the missing pieces of the puzzle, for I knew that one day the kaleidoscope would fall into place, and everything in my experience would become crystal clear. Deep within myself, I waited for such a time, which the Divine Mother assured me would indeed come to pass.

The years rolled by, and my journey continued to unfold. I attended college, where I studied theater arts as well as comparative religion and philosophy. After I graduated, I became successful in my young adult life, and creative expression provided me with an enjoyable career performing. In the late 1960s, the early days of the flower children were at hand, and with the blossoming of the counterculture's interest in the spiritual arena, my mystical expression was ever so appropriate. The spiritual experience was always with me, and I was happy and at peace with myself as I witnessed the great mystery called life.

CHAPTER 2

Journeys to the East

These three things are rare indeed:
a human birth,
the longing for freedom,
and the guidance of an enlightened master.

SHANKARACHARYA, VIVEKACHUDAMINI

By 1970, I had arrived in my midtwenties, and my experience with the photograph of Muktananda that my friends had handed me seemed to hold the potential of finally weaving the pieces of my life into one whole and beautiful tapestry.

In the days following my profound mystical experience while looking at the photograph, I noticed that the divine energy it had awakened remained with me, and I would spontaneously enter into states of suspended thought. Then, enveloped in a profound stillness, transcendental experience would unfold. I did not yet know that this was true meditation, yet I was mesmerized by its manifestation, and I enjoyed its regular occurrence, which always left me intoxicated with bliss and peace.

A week or so later, in the middle of the night, I awakened from a very deep sleep to find the room flooded with divine light. All was bathed in the indigo blue magnificence that always accompanied the manifestation of the Divine Mother, and subtle particles of diamondlike light scintillated and danced everywhere. Like a river flowing into the sea, the luminosity continued to flood the room until all was aglow with divine presence, that intoxicating euphoria that catalyzes awareness and calls attention to the oneness of all that is.

My whole being was filled with ecstasy as this oceanic peace saturated everything. Time was suspended, and from the sacred stillness beyond all boundaries, celestial sounds reverberated. Then I heard the calling of my name, with a maternal magnificence that always remains beyond words yet conveys a love that is absolute and unconditional.

Finally, the form emerged, light condensing and solidifying into shape, a hallucinogenic manifestation that defies all logic yet creates itself as spontaneously and easily as anything known to the rational mind. It was her form, the one I recognized as God as Mother, revealed in all her Godly radiance. Here she was again in celebratory pose, with her head tilted back to the right and arms extended upward to infinity.

Love and love alone flowed between us, the purest love that has no motive and is free in its oneness. Slowly she shifted position and gazed upon me, light reflecting in all directions. As the air filled with the fragrance of millions upon millions of roses and gardenias, she spoke. Her voice echoed through my consciousness: "Go to Muktananda. . . . Muktananda will show you the way."

In silent wonder, I watched as her manifestation lingered, flooding me with a profound love. Then I transcended form, and all manifestation instantly disappeared, replaced with pure awareness. After an hour or so, I emerged from this most sublime state of divine absorption and found myself lying in my bed, numb from head to toe with intoxicating bliss. I recalled the manifestation of the Divine Mother, and her message brought tears to my eyes. I wept uncontrollably, consumed with a love that knows no boundaries, filled with ecstatic gratitude for the answer to my lifelong prayers. For now the mystical guidance that would answer all my questions and deliver me to the fullness of myself had arrived: Muktananda would show me the way.

There was no question whether I would heed the message I had received so clearly. While others might have hesitated before giving up the promising career in performing arts I had begun, or before leaving family, friends, and all that was familiar to travel to a foreign land, for me it did not feel in the least like a sacrifice. All my life, I had experienced a deep spiritual longing, and it was all that really mattered to me. Thus, over the course of the next six months, I began the process of rearranging my affairs so I could journey to the opposite side of the earth in search of this mystical master whose picture had catalyzed such a profound awakening. I unwound myself from my worldly life, including subletting my apartment and extracting myself from my theatrical commitments.

During those months, I located a copy of Muktananda's book, which had just been published in the West, entitled

Guru (currently in print in a revised edition entitled *Play of Consciousness*, South Fallsburg, NY: SYDA Foundation, 1994). Through reading this book, I learned more about Eastern philosophy and the principles of enlightening experience, which helped to put my profound experience upon viewing Muktananda's photograph into perspective, as well as to shed light on my experiences with the Divine Mother since early childhood.

My friends, who used their travels to support their small handicraft business, were planning a trip to North Africa and the East that would include India. They invited me to come along. I agreed, since joining them presented the perfect opportunity for me to fulfill my dreams.

My friends planned a variety of stops on our way to India, including Spain, Morocco, Turkey, and Pakistan, and throughout the course of our journey, I received many signs confirming that I was on the appropriate path. At times it felt as if a hand was resting upon my shoulder, guiding my unfolding experiences.

We arrived in Lisbon, Portugal, from New York, and then traveled down the coast to Cabo de Sao Vicente, which is located at the western corner of Europe, where there is a big lighthouse and small hotel. One night while there, I set out in the light of the full moon to sit on the rocks at the edge of the magnificent five hundred-foot cliffs that dropped to the ocean. In this spectacular setting, with the wind blowing, I once again had a visionary experience in which the Divine Mother appeared, repeating her validation, saying, "Go to Muktananda. . . . Muktananda will show you the way."

As we continued on our journey and arrived in Morocco, we stayed in a small village a few miles from the central city of Fez. The people used to go to the hot springs there, where the grave of a Muslim saint was located, along with a shrine dedicated to him that attracted many pilgrims to pay homage. One night we went up to see the shrine in the moonlight. Sitting there near the grave of the holy man, meditation came over me, and while I was in this spontaneous state the face of the Muslim holy man buried in his grave appeared to me and conveyed who he was. Giving me his blessing, he said to me, "Go to Muktananda. . . . Muktananda will show you the way." This message was coming to me so consistently, and from so many directions, that there was no way I could miss it.

In Istanbul, Turkey, I journeyed to the Blue Mosque, a popular tourist destination as well as a holy shrine in the Muslim tradition. Immediately upon entering the mosque, I was transported by an expanded state of hallucinatory awareness. Once again, I heard the Divine Mother's voice, reiterating her familiar message directing me to Muktananda.

We traveled through Afghanistan and Pakistan, and then spontaneously took a side trip to Sri Lanka. It was by now December, and the Khyber Pass into India was freezing, so we went to a southern port city in Pakistan to arrange travel by boat to Bombay. The travel agent informed us of a special rate on a flight to Sri Lanka. Delighted, we decided to make a slight detour before going to India.

Sri Lanka was a beautiful, magical country with all variety of tropical splendor. We ended up deciding to stay for a time in a small village in the extreme south of the island, where we made friends with many of the villagers as well as the village head. Here, as an astrologer, I was a particularly welcomed and honored guest. For in Sri Lanka, children have their astrological charts written on palm leaves at birth, and astrology is viewed as an ancient art according to the Vedic scriptures. We settled in to enjoy life in this tropical paradise.

After some time, two other Westerners arrived in the town, and the villagers brought them to meet us. These American hippies spent a couple of days with us, and in yet another confirmation of my path, it turned out that their last stop before reaching Sri Lanka had been Muktananda's ashram. This got my attention. Of all the people to find me at the remote end of Sri Lanka, these travelers had just had contact with Muktananda. They gave me a chanting book from his ashram as a gift since I would be going there soon.

A day or so later, I picked up the book, opened its cover, and on the inside page found a photo of Muktananda smiling, with his finger pointing right at me. The caption under the picture read, "Remember—I'm watching." Once again, I entered into an altered state of consciousness, reminiscent of my experience when I had first seen his photo many months before. I heard again the refrain: "Go to Muktananda. . . . Muktananda will show you the way." This reminder signaled to me that it was time to go, so I made the necessary arrangements.

The villagers were heartbroken to see us leave, and threw us a beautiful celebration to bid us farewell. The ceremony included an amazing performance, called devil dancing, in which the performers and the musicians came to our home in the early part of the morning, and spent all day long making their costumes and set out of trees and leaves and palm tree fronds. Then, just after sunset, they guided us to the seats of honor, and two men held a huge sheet up in front of us until the show began. The sheet was dropped, and along with the magnificent set, illumined only with oil lamps, two drummers faced us as they created amazing rhythms with their coconut drums. For the next several hours, through dance and mime, they performed scenes from Buddhist scripture. All of this was done to cleanse and purify us and make us ready before our journey. I found it very interesting that this cleansing ceremony was offered as a farewell gift, when so soon I would be traveling to Muktananda.

From the small village, we made our journey north to the port city of Colombo. Upon arriving in Colombo, I didn't feel well, and soon ended up flat on my back in the hospital for six weeks with hepatitis. Hepatitis involves the liver, and the liver in Eastern philosophy is related to the soul. From an Eastern perspective, the whole process would be considered purification of the soul in preparation for meeting the master. So the devil dancing had worked, unbeknownst to me, and there I was in the hospital and couldn't do anything for six weeks but lie in bed.

In the hospital, I had another one of my mystical experiences. My friends at this point had continued their travels since they had business commitments in India and couldn't do any more for me. They said they'd meet me in the south of India in several weeks' time. One of the nurses at the hospital, who happened to speak English, was very kind to me, and would bring me various books and pamphlets to read and leave them on the bedside table. If I got the strength to read, I would reach over and peruse one of them. At night, a mosquito net was drawn around the bed, and I would go to sleep. Often I would awaken in the night to see a figure standing in front of me outside of the mosquito net. He was wearing an orange robe. At first I thought it must be Muktananda, because I had been told he wore orange robes, but this man's hair looked more like an Afro. He stood there, radiating healing energy. Finally, the nurse brought me some new booklets. I picked one up, and there on the back cover was the man I had been seeing standing at the foot of the bed. His name was Satya Sai Baba. He was very well known as the miracle man of India and was a great guru to hundreds of thousands of devout Hindus. Although he had never left India, he had followers throughout the world, as many Westerners had journeyed to spend time with him.

Some confusion entered my mind as I read about Satya Sai Baba. What had happened to Muktananda? Now there was another holy man appearing to me. The nurse, who was one of his followers, brought me many more books about him. Finally, I was recovered enough to journey to join my friends in India. Satya Sai Baba's ashram was around three and a half hours from Bangalore, where my friends and I were staying, so I considered whether there might be a way for me to meet him. It was now summer in India, and 120 degrees in the shade, and the journey to his ashram was an arduous one. I was still recovering from my illness, and the prospect of such a trip was daunting. But then we discovered that Satya Sai Baba came to an estate on the outskirts of Bangalore for three weeks every summer, and he was there at that very time.

My friends and I went out to meet him, and since he was on vacation, instead of the usual thousands of his followers, a couple of hundred were gathered. He came out to greet people. Without speaking, he moved through the crowd, almost seeming to float along the ground. When I first saw him, the sun was behind him, and the radiance of his energy field was stunning. This was my first experience with an enlightening master in a physical body. I was overwhelmed and ecstatic, and I thought to myself that maybe this was my master. Now, Vedic monks anoint themselves with ash from their fire rituals that has been blessed and imbued with mantras. It is molded into little cakes and dried, and the energetic vibration of this ash is considered to be holy. Satya Sai Baba was known for being able to manifest this ash out of thin air. He would move his hand in a circle and manifest the ash, and then he would pour it into the hand of one of the people gathered to see him. Of course, that person would then share the ash with those around, but it was considered a very auspicious sign to be the recipient.

There I was, sitting in the audience with a couple of hundred people, and he walked over and stopped right in front of me. Then he moved his hand in a circle, produced the ash, and poured it into my hand. He remained silent while others gathered around me as I shared the ash. Again, I wondered whether I was meant to stay with him. I went back and forth about whether I should stay here or go on. My friends encouraged me to ask Satya Sai Baba. I said, "How can I ask him? He doesn't talk." I was told that I could write my question on a piece of paper, and that when he came by, he would take the piece of paper and hold it, and the answer would come. So I wrote the questions "Are you my master? Should I stay here with you?" on a scrap of paper. When Satya Sai Baba came by and took the paper in his hands, my awareness expanded, and I went into the familiar time-warped state of witness consciousness. In a clear voice that I knew was Sai Baba's, I heard the words "Go to Muktananda. . . . Muktananda will show you the way." I had my answer.

Later I came to understand that Satya Sai Baba, who was known for his healing powers, had come into my life at a time of purification, illness, and healing. The symbolism of this experience was completely appropriate in my unfolding journey. After I met with Sai Baba, my medical tests showed that the hepatitis was completely cleared from my system. From that day on, I felt restored to full health. His healing energy completed the purificatory process in preparation for my meeting with Muktananda.

From Satya Sai Baba's, I went straight to Muktananda's ashram. From Bombay, it was a half-day's journey due to the archaic travel conditions, even though it was only seventy-five miles. At the final bus stand, I met a couple of Americans from New York who told me they lived in the ashram and offered to escort me directly there.

As we rounded the final curve in the road toward the ashram, I was amazed at the sight that unfolded before me. Although I had read Muktananda's book, the book had been written about his experiences many years prior, and somehow I had formed in my mind a picture of him meditating in a small hut in relative isolation. I was expecting a small hermitage. I was totally unprepared for the size and scope of his ashram and his following, for in the years since the experiences described in his book, he had become known as a saint and mystical master, and thousands upon thousands, including Indira Gandhi, then the prime minister of India, had come to regard him as their guru.

Arising out of the dry desert of the Indian summer, as we rounded that final curve, I saw before me a lush, green oasis with buildings painted in pale yellows. Palm trees and orange-colored flags swayed in the breeze. Everything was green and abundant and seemed to reflect great wealth as opposed to the simple hut I had anticipated.

I recall standing before the gates to the ashram and realizing that once I entered my life would be forever changed. It was as if there was a choice—and yet at the same time there wasn't a choice. This was my final chance to change my mind, but the pull and the validation to find answers to all my questions at long last were so powerful that it was as if the tide of my whole journey had caught me and carried me to this moment. I hesitated a moment, and then went in.

After waiting for his next appearance, I finally met Muktananda in person for the first time. He welcomed me with love. As he spoke, his powerful presence completely consumed me, and I experienced again the mystical awakening that had come over me when I first saw his photograph in far-off New York. Yet this time it was magnified a hundredfold. I was totally intoxicated on God for the next three days, scaling the heights of ecstasy beyond anything I had yet experienced. This absolute bliss reconfirmed my decision to seek out Muktananda. I knew I had found what I was looking for.

The closest thing in ordinary human life to meeting a true enlightening master is the state of falling in love for the first time, with all the bliss and ecstasy expanded a thousand times over. In the presence of the beloved, all else loses importance. So from the first moments of our contact, I knew that being with Muktananda was all that mattered. I knew I was meant to be his disciple. Thus, I would easily give up career goals, close contact with my family, and for many years the creature comforts of life in the West in order to be near this enlightening master. Truly, for me it was no sacrifice, for just as a lover will give up even riches in order to be near the beloved, so I was willing to do anything to enjoy the bliss of being in Muktananda's enlightening presence. He offered me the opportunity to fulfill my deepest longing.

I stayed on as Muktananda's disciple, both in India and during his many journeys to the West, and the days turned into years, twelve to be exact, until he left his body and merged into the oneness of all that is. During those years of our togetherness, I became one of his closest disciples as well as his personal secretary. He offered a living example of liberated existence as the embodiment of freedom, the ultimate human experience. For that was his name: Muktananda, the bliss of freedom. He manifested the bliss of freedom not only in his words and teachings but in his day-to-day actions. Muktananda lived his truth, and this is how he catalyzed my own radical expansion of awareness. He never ceased to exemplify the reality of the human God, and he inspired all he encountered to become the same as himself.

For Muktananda, all was but a play of consciousness, the awareness of which liberated a human being from the illusory bondage that there could ever be anything else. His state of being emanated the most powerful presence one could ever imagine. Just as lower frequencies entrain other frequencies to their level, the master's energy field experientially entrained all that came into contact with it to the same awareness of God, or Source. Within Muktananda's environment, there was no doubt that existence itself was God and God alone, the one without a second.

Little did I know when I first heard Muktananda's name that the answer to all my questions was contained therein, a seed pregnant with the truth of all life—that freedom is all there is, and true freedom is always blissful. So, indeed, I came to Muktananda, and Muktananda showed me the way.

Before Muktananda died, he told me to return to my country and share the ancient and eternal experience of the truth of all life. He asked me to find a way to take this experience beyond the difference of cultures and religious traditions, and to express the one truthful awareness that transcends yet includes all existence. For the last fifteen years, I have endeavored to actualize his wishes as my journey continues to unfold in all its unified diversity, and I am fulfilled in each moment. Now I share how I arrived within this moment, for it is a glorious moment. It is the moment beyond all moments and including all moments. It is oneness. It is truth. It is God. It is Source. . . . It is the bliss of freedom.

PART ONE

SOURCE

I am
Here . . . now
Transcendental, immanent
A unity in diversity
One Source celebrating itself
Forever delighting
Eternally playing
Being and becoming
Pure awareness
The bliss of freedom

CHAPTER 3

The True Nature of Reality

The essence and the whole of all philosophy
is this awareness, this supreme awareness,
that I am Source.

AVADHUT GITA

At some point in their lives, almost all human beings ask the fundamental questions: What's it all about? Why am I here? What is the meaning and purpose of life? We find ourselves in the midst of the human journey, and we have to figure it out as we go along. We use everything available to us to answer these important questions, and all of our experience is included in the solutions we propose. Along with our own personal journey, we are influenced by the journeys of various individuals before us, and the collective journey of the whole of humanity down through the ages. Early on, it becomes obvious that we are here to learn. But what exactly are we supposed to learn? If we allow our focus to become like a laser, perhaps what we are really asking is: What is the true nature of reality?

Considering that so many have taken this journey before us, there is a wealth of information available to guide us on our path, the examination of which reveals a common thread. From the most ancient cultures to the present, all philosophical traditions are based on it. True reality, ultimate reality, is one and single. It is nondual. It includes all and everything, both manifest and unmanifest, and it is also forever beyond all such distinctions. Whether it is called *reality, intelligence, consciousness, truth,* or *the force,* it is the same. Many people call it *God.* Through the centuries, such a vast divergence of human interpretation has been projected onto this tiny, three-letter word. With all this entangled confusion and contradiction, there is rarely agreement on what exactly God is. Is God form or formlessness? Is God one or many? Can God be known or does God remain unknown? So the debate continues even in our own time.

Considering all the paradox, it is difficult to communicate clearly on the subject, for first we have to wade through a morass of conceptual differences. The whole process simply becomes too frustrating for most people to pursue it very far. We have even had to separate the whole subject of God from the affairs of state, or nothing would ever have been accomplished beyond religious conflict.

Given all this, I decided long ago that I didn't like using the three-letter word *God,* because for the most part it no longer had anything to do with truthful reality. I chose a new word, a word free from the conceptual bondage that had compromised the word *God.* I chose the word *Source:* Source, the fundamental essence of all that is, the ultimate reality, transcendent and immanent, manifest and unmanifest, the totality of what is and what is not, the forever beyond, a unity in diversity, the one without a second.

This choice emerged from my own personal experience during my formative years. The Roman Catholic tradition in which I was reared espoused a horrific God who judged people for all that they did and punished them for most of it. Everyone was supposed to live according to a set of rules and regulations that no one except saints could truly master. As far as I could see, according to this perspective almost everyone was going to hell, because the criteria for heavenly admittance were virtually impossible to fulfill.

The problem was that hell, fire, and damnation were not at all congruent with what I was experiencing in the soft and ethereal darkness of my very real bedroom almost every night. The God that I experienced was alive, luminous, beautiful, loving, compassionate, peaceful, and ecstatic. It was Source celebrating its own magnificence, free and joyful. Source presented itself to me as a delightful, playful, and magical reality.

Since our beliefs influence our perception of reality, I first manifested God according to my religious conditioning as the Virgin Mother of Christianity. I readily accepted this form as God, and yet what she taught me was completely different from what Christianity was trying to teach me. This Motherly God expressed the eternal delight of existence, the sacredness of all life, and the celebration of life as play for the pure fun of it. She showed me that life was a game to be played for the joy of it, just as children play games with no goal other than their own laughter. This was life without stress, without limiting belief. It was life lived with freedom.

Mystics down through the ages have used storytelling to communicate in the most easily understandable ways the intricacies of the true nature of Sourceful reality. From the myths of the Vedic seers through the chronicles of

Buddha and the parables of Christ, to the anecdotes of a modern Muktananda, simple human stories render abstruse philosophical principles into human expressions that everyone can relate to and understand.

Muktananda was a master storyteller. He brought us to both tears and laughter day after day as he diligently delineated the ancient and eternal principles of conscious living. His dialogues were in the classical Vedic style, which is always permeated with stories and quotations from the writings of great enlightening sages. He taught me to speak in this style as well. Over the years, I have collected many stories and regularly use them in my program presentations.

One of my favorite of these stories pointing to the truthful understanding of Source I call "The Monk and the Milk Story." Once upon a time, some monks lived in a monastery. In those days, there were both male and female renunciants who shared a monastic life together. Every day, they went out into the nearby village, and the villagers would put food into their begging bowls. They would bring this food back to the monastery and enjoy their meal. One of the brothers was a very enlightening monk who was very expanded in his awareness. One day, as this brother was crossing the village square with his begging bowl in hand, he encountered a fight going on. A landlord was abusing his tenant. Their words became more intense, and suddenly the landlord knocked the tenant to the ground.

The enlightening brother, being very compassionate, took up the plight of the tenant, whereupon the landlord knocked the monk unconscious to the ground. Of course, everyone was all upset, and word went back to the monastery, and all the brothers and sisters came. They placed the monk on a stretcher and carried him back to the monastery, where they laid him on his bed. One of them said, "Quick, quick, quick. Go and bring some milk. We'll try to revive him and see if he can recognize who is feeding him." So they brought the milk to the brother, who was just regaining consciousness, and they gathered around the bed to give it to him, trying to force him to drink it. "Brother, brother," they said, "are you aware of who is giving you this milk to drink?" Whereupon the enlightening brother replied, "Yes, I am. He who beat me now gives me this milk to drink."

This story so beautifully captures the enlightening brother's awareness of the unity of essence. A Sanskrit verse from the ancient Tantric text the Vijnana Bhairava ("The Nature of God") rendered into English expresses the same nondual truth and once again demonstrates that for thousands of years human beings have explored a truthful understanding of the nature of reality. It simply states, "The same consciousness is present in all and everything. There is no difference in it anywhere. A person realizing that everything is the same consciousness is triumphantly liberated." Once again the point is clearly stated: If you are filled with Source awareness, which is nondual, you will not experience the world as something separate from you, nor exclude one experience while embracing another. In enlightening awareness, there is no subject and no object; all are the same consciousness, expressing the unity in diversity of Source.

In yet another story, from the Zen tradition, we find a reiteration of the same theme. It concerns a mendicant who lived in a little hut on the top of a mountain in the middle of nowhere, engaged in a simple life of meditation and enlightening awareness. He didn't have much in his little hut because he was a mendicant, and aside from a small teapot and his clothes and some basic utensils, he had few worldly possessions. One day this enlightening mendicant returned to his hut after a journey, and encountered a thief who had just arrived to steal whatever he could. The thief was frightened at being discovered, but the monk was not like anyone else whose house was being robbed.

He immediately had compassion for the thief, and he said to him, "Here you are! You've come all this way, and you've gone to all this trouble, and there's nothing here for you to take. I have nothing. I feel so sorry for you." And with these words, he undressed and gave the thief the clothes off his back. And he added, "Take these clothes. Then at least your journey will not have been in vain." The thief didn't know what to make of this, and he left in bewilderment with the clothes. By now it was early evening, and the full moon was rising, so the monk, absolutely naked, came out to sit on the side of the mountain to watch the spectacle. As the heavenly orb rose over the horizon, he said to himself, "Ah, if only I could give him this moon!"

Again, this story points to a freedom that goes beyond duality. The enlightening mendicant clearly understood the true nature of reality. The Avadhut Gita, an ancient Indian mystic's writing whose title translates as "Song of the Ecstatic," puts it this way: "Source is like the full moon. See it in all. Duality is the product of delusion. As there is only one moon, there is only one Source."

Cross-culturally, the stories flow one after another, tracking our human exploration of the true nature of reality.

Here is one from the Taoist tradition. It seems there was a
monk who was an assistant to the master of a monastery.
One day the master of the monastery said to him that he
would like something different for lunch. The assistant
monk ran to the kitchen and said, "Go to the market and
fetch the best vegetable for Master's dinner." The cook, all
excited at the opportunity to serve his master, ran down to
the marketplace to one of the brothers from the monastery
who ran a vegetable stand. Now this brother happened to
be very enlightening and blissful. "Quick, quick, I must
have the best vegetable for Master's lunch," the cook
called out. Whereupon the enlightening brother replied,
"Everything is best."

As an old aphorism goes: A fool once searched for fire
with a flaming lantern in his hand. If he had known what
fire was, he could have cooked his rice much sooner! So,
as story after story elucidates, in the human journey of expanding awareness we learn that who we are looking for is
who is looking. Within the diversity of manifest existence,
the same Source expresses itself. As Shankaracharya, an
enlightening sage believed to be a direct incarnation of
God who revitalized Hinduism many centuries ago, said
in his treatise the Vivekachudamini, "As an actor when he
is with costume or without is always a man, so the perfect
knower of Source is always Source and nothing else."

Indeed, to experience Source is to be Source. Source is
not an object. It is who we are—one with all that is. To understand this is to enter the bliss of freedom. Even modern science affirms this awareness. Fritjof Capra, in his
book *The Tao of Physics*, writes: "In modern physics, the
universe is thus experienced as a dynamic, inseparable
whole which always includes the observer in an essential
way. In this experience, the traditional concepts of space

and time, of isolated objects, and of cause and effect, lose their meaning. Such an experience is very similar to that of the Eastern mystics." In the Ashtavakra Gita ("The Song of Ashtavakra"), the sage Ashtavakra puts it thus: "Just as waves and bubbles are not different from water, even so Source expressing the universe is not different from it." The essence of all the stories and quotations is the simple truth that authentic enlightening masters live constantly in this nondual awareness, and share it with all who enter their energy field.

CHAPTER 4

The Eternal Delight of Being

Because of the awareness that everything is Source,
one remains the same in all dualities,
and because of this awareness
is forever blissful.

VIJNANA BHAIRAVA

Within the first few weeks of my arrival at Muktananda's Indian ashram, I continued to experience the most amazing manifestations of the reality that I had come to call Source. Muktananda appeared publicly several times each day to greet the many who came to honor his presence and receive his blessing. He sat in the courtyard within the central compound of the ashram, and received long lines of people who presented him with their traditional offerings of colorful flower garlands, brown coconuts, pungent incense sticks, sumptuous fruit, and other gifts. They touched his feet and experienced his Godliness, for this was normal within their culture: the honoring of the living mystical master.

For those of us who resided in the ashram, these spontaneous appearances usually happened during our time of

43

service, which included office work, kitchen work, cleaning duties, and gardening. In the course of our duties, if we were passing through the courtyard where Muktananda was receiving the visiting pilgrims, we were permitted to remain and enjoy his blissful presence.

One day I found myself in the courtyard during one of his morning sessions. I was standing at the back about a hundred feet from Muktananda. I was focused on him, just watching, as he received one after another with love. All of a sudden, energy exploded within me and quickly expanded to its peak, rushing outward from the center of my being and flooding all dimensions. As I gazed at him, he looked directly into my eyes and smiled to acknowledge the exchange. A few minutes later, he looked at me again and winked. Each such exchange expanded my energy field, and I began to hallucinate. Everything undulated with waves of ecstatic consciousness.

I continued to focus upon him, and my eyes and body locked into that position. Then he disappeared, and I saw only blue light in place of his form. Then he reappeared, only to disappear again a moment or two later, to be replaced by a brightly burning flame the size of his body. Then he reappeared and then disappeared as the Divine Mother appeared in his place, in the same posture she always assumed, with her hands thrown back in abandoned ecstasy. Then she was gone, and he was back again.

By this time, the energy was so intense that I was holding myself with both my arms wrapped around my body, because I felt that if I did not hold myself together I would surely explode into a million pieces. I felt I was on the edge of losing my mind, and that if I could not contain the energy I would soon be hauled off by those proverbial men in the white coats. I thought I was about to go insane. I had never been this expanded while physically conscious, and I was filled with both ecstasy and fear. I could only remain a witness without any control over what was happening, and my mind was racing away. Just at the most intense peak of this experience, Muktananda stood up to leave. As he did so, he looked directly at me again, nodded with a smile, and then turned and left the courtyard. My energy surged again, and I was even more frightened. I stood there immobilized.

Muktananda's translator was also exiting the courtyard, and he happened to pass right by me. He noticed my situation, and asked if I was all right. He seemed a million miles away, at the end of a long tunnel of light. I didn't respond. I couldn't, because my body was still locked. He asked again, and immediately the lock was relinquished, and I came rushing back into physical focus. Still holding myself, I told him that I didn't think I was all right, and I tried to explain my state and my fear. He helped me to a nearby seat, and comforted me by telling me not to worry but to just sit and watch. When Muktananda returned, he told me, we would consult with him about it.

An hour passed, and the energy I was experiencing remained constant. Undulating waves of luminous consciousness moved in all directions. I was simultaneously drunk with bliss and frightened as Muktananda returned to the courtyard. After he greeted those who were waiting to see him, the translator motioned me forward. He translated while I explained how I felt. Muktananda smiled. Taking my hand in his, he explained that I was experiencing an appropriate transmission of Source in the presence of the master, and that I was very blessed to experience it.

He said that I was able to receive this transmission due to my purity, and explained that many came to him seeking this experience in vain, for it was not yet their time. Nevertheless, here I was from the other side of the world, and both through his photograph and his physical presence, I was experiencing his energy transmission.

Muktananda validated my experience, and all my fear diminished. He was still holding my hand, and the energy dynamic was increasing gradually. With the fear gone, I became more and more blissful, at first to the point of face-consuming smiles, and then to light laughter. He began to laugh, too, and told me to relax, release, and let the laughter happen. Then I began to laugh myself right out of control. As I did so, he said that this was happening because I had never truly laughed before. He directed me to the upper gardens and said I should find a rock to sit on, and remain there until I stopped laughing. We continued to laugh together for another few minutes, and then I started my journey to the upper garden.

All the way I could not stop laughing. Everything seemed so funny. All was but a joke with no seriousness whatsoever anywhere to be found. I remained in this state of blissful awareness and observed the many dimensions of phenomenal manifestation. Everything was so beautiful, bathed in the indigo-colored light that I had come to recognize as Source. Yet in these moments, all form was expressing its innate delight in being. As I walked along, the stones beneath my feet said, "I love you," and I could feel their love rippling throughout the subtlest dimensions of my being. The trees, the air, the sun in the sky, and the whole of nature reverberated with the same loving delight. Together they sounded a rapturous symphony of oneness celebrating itself. I continued to laugh and laugh, rejoicing in the absolute joy of all existence.

I gradually made my way to the upper garden and found a grouping of rocks in the shade of some generously large mango trees, where I could sit uninterrupted and continue my laughter. I could not stop laughing, and as the hours passed, I laughed on into the darkness of the first night. I missed dinner because I could not stop laughing, and I reasoned that eating was unimportant. I was not hungry anyway, for I was filled to capacity with energy, and all appetite had long since disappeared.

I continued laughing, and the whole of my life began to pass before me, as if I were watching a movie. I saw all the roles I had played, all the costumes I had worn, all the different faces superimposed over my original face, all the dimensions overlaying the original dimension of essence. I was a boy, an adolescent, a young man. I was a son, a grandchild, a cousin, a friend, a lover, a religious person, an entertainer, a flower child. And so on. I was merged in the reality of Source, and I observed everything as masks, dimension after dimension, hiding the original truth, yet manifesting for the sheer fun of it, creating a game of hide-and-seek within itself, for the sake of itself, for its own eternal entertainment.

From this perspective, everything was ever so silly and funny, especially those masks that were the most serious, and this awareness made me laugh all the more. I saw everyone I had ever known, and all the roles they had played with me. Then I saw the roles of the whole of humanity playing simultaneously one against the other, one within the other. It was farcical, a slapstick comedy of divine proportions, a theater of the absurd without reason or purpose, just entertainment for entertainment's sake. Life, the whole of existence, was just a Sourceful play, and there was absolutely nothing serious about it at all.

Before I knew it, the sun was rising, and I was still laughing. My sides were aching, yet I couldn't stop laughing, for it was all just too delightfully funny. It crossed my mind that I should eat some breakfast, but I quickly abandoned the idea because the thought of eating was also funny and produced even more laughter. After a while, some of my fellow disciples came to check on me. They had heard of my experience and came to see for themselves. They gathered around the rock where I was sitting and soon began to laugh with me, for the laughter was infectious. My energy had become so full of Source that everyone became intoxicated with bliss, and we laughed on and on together. After a while, they left to return to their duties, and I remained there on my own, laughter into laughter, bliss into bliss.

I had never been so high and so free. All stress had left my being, and, once again, I was like an eagle floating upon the wind beyond all cares and concerns, lost in the reality of Source. There was love and love alone. I was free within the oneness of all that is, and that was all that mattered.

Another day passed, and by lunchtime of the third day, I thought I should really try to get something to eat. I was not at all hungry, but the conditioned thought that food was needed for survival kept surfacing in my mind. I decided to try to control my laughter, get to the dining hall for lunch, and then return to the rock. I managed to suppress the laughter while I walked to the dining hall, but no sooner had I sat down than I burst once more into hysterical laughter, causing a great commotion. I ran out of the hall, laughing all the way back to my rock in the upper garden. The whole incident filled me with such amusement that I laughed all the more for the next day and a half.

By nighttime, I began to think I should try to sleep. Again, I was not the least bit tired, but the conditioned thought about sleep being necessary for survival was overpowering. No sooner did I lie down in the dormitory than laughter erupted yet again, waking all around me from their sleep. I ran out and returned to my rock. This, too, was so incredibly funny that I laughed even harder for the next few days.

Finally, I abandoned all thought whatsoever, for nothing really mattered. There was only the laughter. My mind became still and silent, and the pure awareness of myself as blissful Source filled the whole of my being. The intensity of the physical laughter was relaxing now, yet every particle of my being was engaged in the laughter. It was a self-fulfillment throughout all levels of awareness, a contentment that was in want of nothing, an enjoyment in the pure delight of being. Everything was just as it should be.

By the tenth day, I was resigned to spending the rest of my life on that rock, for nothing I had ever experienced seemed more truthful or more real. I was totally relaxed and at one with my universe, just witnessing the laughing delight of all and everything.

As I was lying down across the biggest rock and laughing lightly, Muktananda came along the path with his translator to see me. He stood there for a few moments silently gazing upon me. Then he inquired how I was doing. I could not speak because I felt totally overwhelmed with love for him. I just wept and laughed at the same time, as the by-now-familiar words echoed in the depths of my being: "Muktananda will show you the way."

He called me to him and embraced me. Stroking my head and upper back, he told me that he was pleased with me, and repeated that this was my home and I must stay and meditate intensely. Gradually, the laughter diminished and stopped. Looking me in the eyes, his own eyes reflecting all the laughter of all the universe, he said, "Now you are truly laughing." Gratitude filled my heart, and I bowed at his feet, filled with a love no words could ever describe and consumed in the dynamic ecstasy that only disciples know when they have found an authentic mystical master.

CHAPTER 5

Meditation Opens the Door

Because the individual soul is identical
with the whole universe, hence,
whether in word, object, or mental apprehension,
there is no state that is not God.
Awareness of this truth alone constitutes freedom.
Want of it constitutes bondage.

VASAGUPTA, SPANDAKARIKA

Muktananda used to tell a story about how his master had
taught him and catalyzed his own ever-evolving illumination. He told us that he used to be addicted to reading
books, particularly scriptures and philosophy, and that this
consumed most of his time. One night, shortly after he
had met his master, he was sitting in the main reception
room of his master's ashram reading a philosophy book.
The master had retired for the night, and Muktananda
thought he was alone. Without warning, the master entered the room, walked over to Muktananda, and asked,
"What are you doing?" "I am reading this book," Muktananda replied. The master then said, "Don't you understand? Minds make books; books don't make minds."

51

Muktananda got the point: that you can't reach illumination by reading about it, or thinking about it, for it is far greater than the mind; it is beyond the mind. Muktananda told us that he abandoned reading after that incident, and devoted himself to meditation and the beyond-the-mind experience. This became the way he taught me and everyone else: experience first, conceptual understanding thereafter. Once we had immersed ourselves in the experience, then and only then would he teach us the philosophy that had emerged from such experience down through the ages. This was a particularly difficult practice for Westerners, who tend to place so much importance on the mind. Muktananda even kept the ashram library locked, and until you had tasted direct experience, you could not get any books to read. All reading and study were for a greater elucidation of the direct experience.

Since my relationship with Muktananda was very close, he guided me personally in the journey. At times he taught me directly from the ancient scriptures and related philosophical systems himself, and at other times he assigned me to various pundits and experts. Yet each principle remained based on direct experience first, and explanation or delineation second. He placed great emphasis on the documented accounts of other human beings who had experienced mystical truths in their lives throughout history. This facilitated a well-rounded understanding.

Meditation, however, stood first and foremost, the heart of the inner, experiential journey of personal exploration and discovery, the journey beyond the mind, the journey of Source. Truly, Source is like a misty rain, falling softly but flooding the river, and meditation opens us to this awareness.

From my own meditation experience, I learned the true nature of reality, the nature of Source, and this was validated by all I was given to study. From the most ancient delineations, Source is described as that which is absolutely one and free. It is nondual reality, both manifest, unmanifest, and forever beyond. It is pure awareness. To manifest itself for its own delight, pure awareness polarizes itself into a seeming duality, the play of opposites, and through the stress of imbalance densifies itself into the universal creation. Yet it remains a unity in diversity, a nondual reality playing as a seeming duality for the pure joy of it. It is a free and independent whole, aware of itself existing, giving rise to the eternal delight of being. It is peaceful because it is without stress. It is life as intrinsic celebration. It plays a game of hide-and-seek with itself for the eternal fun of it.

As the illusory opposites condense, stress increases, awareness contracts, and what is really only one appearing as two is perceived as two, the illusion of duality. Perception is distorted through the mind with its limited, dualistic beliefs. So most human beings hold onto the perceived reality of the duality of opposites, the separation of subject and object. Devoid of truthful awareness, this perspective is also limited in delight. This misperception leads to the world of pain and suffering. Yet from the perspective of true reality, it is all just a game for the fun of it, and ultimately Source reveals itself to itself, relinquishes dual illusion, and awareness celebrates itself as absolute freedom.

From the limited perception of most human beings, what you think is what you get. Their beliefs distort their reality, and what they perceive is mostly unconscious illusion. The key to liberation is the relinquishment of fraudulent beliefs, accomplished through the expansion of true, Sourceful awareness. This awareness arises from moving beyond the mind through the mastery of the mind, the stilling of it. The most ancient technique in this progressive process of mind mastery is meditation.

Through meditation, we transcend the dualistic data of our mind, transmuting it to truthful, nondual data, and ultimately passing beyond the mind and all data into pure awareness. This is the journey to unity consciousness, with the proportional expansions of awareness along the way. This is a journey from here to here, for in the process, time and space are truthfully perceived as illusion. There is only the eternal now, the simultaneity of all existence, beyond duality, without beginning or end, the play of consciousness unto forever.

The human journey entails an expansion of awareness that all is one reality, a unity in diversity, the ultimate realization that even you, as a human being, are this manifest God, this celebrating Source. This realization is experienced as the nondual mind becomes quiescent in the awareness of itself and all that is as one Source, one existence, one reality that is total and inclusive. The meditative experience involves a progressive clearing and expansion of this awareness. It is an ever-expanding freedom. As one Zen koan puts it, "You must not try to catch Source in the way you perceive a star, a tree, or a table before you. To know that is to know that to know is not to know, and that not to know is to know. Because it is ungraspable, it is graspable; because it is un-understandable, it is understandable."

My own personal meditative experience kept expanding throughout my years with Muktananda. Living in his enlightening presence consistently evoked a meditative awareness. Again, this paralleled the scientific process of entrainment. Within the presence of his energy field, deeply transcendental experiences unfolded regularly. I was experiencing ever more expanded dimensions of Source every day. I was becoming blissfully free.

My proximity to Muktananda was a privilege and afforded many profound mystical opportunities. For several years, I was his personal secretary and responsible for the administration of daily organizational business. My role as his secretary had come about seemingly by chance, in yet another one of those synchronicities that guided my destiny.

When Muktananda came to the West on one of his first lengthy tours in the United States, I was there in the San Francisco Bay Area to greet him. It so happened that the tour coordinator's temporary secretary could no longer continue in her role, and the tour coordinator needed someone to type and take dictation. Because I possessed these skills, I was selected for the job.

The office where I worked was directly under Muktananda's bedroom, and I was delighted to have manifested this way of being near his energy field. As things evolved, the tour coordinator, who was somewhat disorganized, required more and more help with the day-to-day organization of the tour, and my role soon expanded to that of assistant. There were logistical problems with the part of the tour planned for the New York area, and I was sent ahead to assist with arrangements. This also gave me an opportunity to tie up more of my personal affairs there.

Muktananda's tour to New York was very successful, and as his stay neared an end, he sent someone to inform me that he would like me to become his personal secretary. Of course, I leapt at this opportunity to be involved intimately in the day-to-day level of his life. Besides handling his correspondence with Westerners, I also helped attend to administrative details entailed in the creation and running of a large religious organization and in the frequent international tours Muktananda embarked upon to spend time with his followers around the world. In addition, I often served as "man Friday," engaging in any kind of immediate task that needed doing.

Once while I was engaged as Muktananda's secretary, he decided to enjoy a period of silence and seclusion. He simply announced one day without warning that he would be sequestered and that no business would be addressed until further notice. I dutifully obeyed his wish for the first week, but when business had piled up to staggering proportions, with letters to answer and administrative details to attend to, I requested to see him and have it addressed. I reasoned that he wouldn't have to talk; he could just nod his head yes or no to a few very simple questions. The whole process should not take very long at all. Eventually, after repeated requests, I was called to his room. He had been silent and secluded for over a week, and his energy field had expanded radically and pervaded the entire ashram.

As I entered his room, I saw him lying on his bed absolutely still and motionless. His eyes were closed in a deep transcendental serenity. He was almost transparent within a white luminous aura that radiated from the center of his being. As was traditional, I proceeded to kneel down to bow my head to the floor before sitting on the floor to address the business. As my knees touched the floor, my

awareness expanded, and the whole room became a swirling, dancing ocean of light and color. The multidimensionality of Source revealed itself in the moment, and the
whole environment reverberated with the echoing refrain:
"God . . . God . . . God . . . I am God. . . . All is God. . . .
God . . . God . . . God." I was intoxicated into oblivion as
everything merged and dissolved, ecstasy into ecstasy, light
into light, Source into Source. From the subtlest dimensions of witness consciousness, I observed my body continue in the motion of its bowing. Yet as my head was about
to touch the floor, the floor disappeared, and all boundaries
merged and dissolved. I fell right through the floor into an
awareness beyond all limitation. I became the reverberating refrain: "God . . . God . . . God . . . I am God. . . . All is
God. . . ." Beyond the words, I was merged and absorbed
in the experience itself. There was only the liberating ecstasy of unlimited existence.

I don't recall being helped back to my room, where I returned to my normal waking awareness several hours later.
I just remember coming back again into my body from the
most expanded dimensions of oneness. The blissful awareness of Source danced within every cell in my body, and
its luminous refractions delighted throughout the room. I
lay there for a long time, watching and celebrating oneness, and then I drifted into sleep for the night, the ethereal strains still echoing within me.

Many enlightening beings throughout history have
shared their experience of absorption into the oneness of
Source. This is particularly well delineated in the philosophical traditions of the East. Mere conceptual description,

however, will not allow you to understand exactly what this experience is. Meditation opens the door to the direct human experience termed *transcendental*. Eventually, through meditation, the polarity of opposites is transcended, and pure unitive awareness is experienced. This total merging is the ultimate human experience of Source.

In a progressive meditative experience, the mind is focused and awareness of Source expands. As the stress of opposites diminishes, the freedom of a deeply peaceful relaxation unfolds, and you become blissful in the awareness of the oneness of all that is. Anyone who has ever experienced this state describes it with words such as *blissful, intoxicating, rapturous, ecstatic*. While the English language contains a smaller vocabulary for describing this state than, for example, Sanskrit, a language richer in its capacity to describe the many subtle dimensions of mystical experience, the essential experience is one and the same. As awareness of Source continues its expansion, it reaches the point of equilibration between the manifest and the unmanifest. This is the balanced still point before everything disappears. As one crosses this threshold, all form vanishes, and only pure awareness remains, the emptiness of the forever beyond.

Those rare human beings who experience such dimensions of truthful reality are considered truly liberated. They are the forever free. Through the mastery of the human experience of Source, they have become mystical masters who are ever constant in this awareness. They are not referred to as *enlightening* because of what they say, but rather because of what they are, because of what others experience in their presence, the radiance of their Source-field, as I like to call it. Enlightening human beings manifest a vibration that reverberates with the minimal stress level at the threshold between the manifest and the unmanifest. Since all human beings are energy forms and all energy vibrates according to its level of innate stress, or lack of stress, all are interrelated by the frequency of their vibrations. The form that embodies minimal stress through maximum balance becomes an entrainment for all in its environment. It automatically draws everyone and everything like a magnet to its awareness of Source. It reflects the resonance of Source beyond all mental manipulation. Such human beings unceasingly enjoy a truthful perception of reality, and they are free in the eternal now of oneness.

The progressive stages of meditative absorption must be demonstrated. Ultimately, one must be shown the way by an adept who has become constant in the experience. Thereafter, one also becomes constant in the experience. Yet, throughout the journey, until its culmination in constancy, the demonstrated example of enlightening mastery is most important. Muktananda was such a mystical master for me through the final twelve years of his life, and without his daily example, it would have been virtually impossible for me to have journeyed through the dimensions of Source that I experienced. He was always showing the way, no matter the situation.

Once, it was the Christmas season and we were in residence at Muktananda's ashram in India. Since Muktananda had an increasingly large Western following, we celebrated such major holidays as Christmas and the New Year. On Christmas Eve morning, he called me to his room. As I entered, he was sitting cross-legged on his bed, as was his custom. His bed was the center of his universe. It was the only major piece of furniture that he consistently used. He slept in it, of course, and he also sat upon it and conducted business throughout the day. Those of us who were close enough to gain access to this inner sanctuary sat on the floor. On this occasion, I noticed that he had something lying across his lap. When I had settled myself on the floor, he showed it to me and explained that it was a musical instrument called a veena. He asked me if I liked it, and I responded that it was very beautiful. It was a stringed instrument composed of a gourd and finely finished wood inlaid with mock ivory. He strummed the veena a few times, and it produced a most meditative sound. The sound was familiar to me, for I had often heard it combined with other sounds in my meditative experiences over the years. "This is for you. It is a Christmas present," he said. The veena had been beautifully handcrafted by one of his Indian disciples and was very special indeed. Muktananda proceeded to show me how to play it.

As was usual, he was in a very elevated state of awareness, and his intoxicatingly peaceful presence was particularly pronounced. His room was always saturated with his energy field, but this day it seemed especially powerful. He began strumming the veena and played it for a few minutes. Then he said, "Whenever you play this instrument, make sure that you are constant in the awareness of your oneness with it." He continued to strum and then began to sing some poetic verses from one of his favorite Indian mystics. From his own state of oneness, he swiftly entrained me, and in an instant we were merged together in the awareness of that oneness.

My awareness skyrocketed upward and outward in all directions, and the phenomenal play of consciousness was everywhere manifest. From the witnessing center of my being, I could hear Muktananda singing and playing the veena, yet it was echoing and mingling with the most ethereal, celestial sound imaginable. Its beauty was so overwhelming that it filled me with love to the peaking point and beyond. All was scintillating indigo-colored luminosity saturated with peace, love, and bliss. The rapturous intoxication was so intense that I knew I would soon disappear, and in the twinkling of an eye it happened. Muktananda and I merged and became one reality delighting in itself, an awareness forever unlimited.

We remained suspended in this state of pure Source awareness and delighted in the absolute bliss of freedom, beyond time, beyond space, beyond all form—the formless, attributeless, one without a second. Then we manifested, and the phenomenal world appeared as we found ourselves embodied in his room once again. He was still playing the veena and singing, and I was blissfully listening, suspended in the shimmering play of witness consciousness. He fell silent for a few minutes as the last reverberation of the strings faded into forever. Gazing into my eyes, he conveyed a love that is only ever shared by those who have experienced the ultimate truth, the one Source that is all and everything. Tears flowed from our eyes in mutual acknowledgment, and our hearts were filled to overflowing with oneness. He handed me the instrument and ever so softly whispered, "Remember . . . remember . . . this is how you play it."

In these ways, over the years of my discipleship, Muktananda entrained my evolving awareness and progressively
guided my mystical journey in his most masterful manner.
The magnificence of our magical relationship continued
to flower, day after day, year after year, and even continues in this moment although he is no longer embodied. It
has been some twenty years since the experiences I am
now sharing took place. What is my current experience of
that which I call Source? This I am also happy to share.

Here and now, in this very moment, as I gaze upon these
words that I am writing, I am aware that they are but the play
of Source, and I am merged in its unitive oneness. Everything constantly undulates with indigo-colored luminescence, and scintillating, diamondlike particles of white
light are eternally delighting, a celebration of Source
within itself. This emanates from the center of my being
and radiates through all dimensions to infinity. It is the
play of one equality consciousness, and in its absolute oneness it is forever free. I am intoxicated with Source as every
cell of my body and all of my multidimensional being reverberates its oneness. I am high on life lived in the awareness of the ultimate truth, that there is but Source and
Source alone. Coming, going, eating, sleeping, walking,
sitting, talking, or listening, I continue my celebration of
Source in the unbroken awareness of true reality. I have
become the bliss of freedom.

Yet, I still do not believe in God—at least not in the limited reality that has been projected upon this tiny three-
letter word. For such limitation is not my experience.
Rather, it is the confused and fraudulent beliefs of unconscious human beings, projected upon an illusory reality through which they give themselves authority to

perpetuate their dualistic madness, and suffer the consequences of their unaware actions. It is a manipulated God, a distorted God, and a limited God that they create in illusory separation, that they might journey and find a greater truth, an eternally unlimited truth, unbeknownst to themselves, that will end their unconscious game of hide-and-seek, and ultimately deliver them to true and lasting freedom.

For me there is no God separate and aloft in the heavens, different from you and me, no matter by what name it is called. No God that could ever say it is better than another God, or different from anyone or anything, for no God that is dualistic can ever be ultimate, can ever be truly real. No God that sets one human being against another, one religion against another, one race or one nation against another, is ever real. For truly, there is no other. This is my experience. In the subtle dimensions of my meditations, I have experienced both the Western Christian God as Mother and the Eastern Vedic God as Mother. Just as I manifested Source as the Divine Mother in my bedroom as a small child, so I have manifested the Buddha, Christ, Krishna, and Mohammed, too, and they have shown me that they are all one, that all are the same Source, a unity in diversity. They have all expressed the same truth, the same oneness, and by dissolving into it have revealed the way beyond all limitation to the ultimate experience of pure awareness, wherein there is but the bliss of freedom, eternal and truthful unto forever.

I continue to manifest that which in the past I have called God as Mother, or the Divine Mother. I no longer view her as something separate from myself, neither as a Christian/Catholic virgin nor as a religious goddess, but as a manifestation of my multidimensional self. For, as the feminine principle of creative expression, she is the ultimate form that I manifest before all form dissolves into the unmanifest void of pure awareness. She is that dimension of myself in which I am manifest as one. She is the play of consciousness that I perceive in each moment. She and I are one. In this manifestation, I am Source.

Today, in my morning meditation, I manifested her form again, and we enjoyed a blissful dialogue about what I am writing in this book in these very moments. She is nourishing, loving, compassionate, and caring. She is the ultimate Mother with the whole of her creation as her child, and she is not different from it. She is oneness having a dialogue with itself for the love of itself. She is the celebration of the one without a second, and when our dialogue is complete, we merge again into the pure awareness of absolute freedom.

Since I am perceiving all that is through this human form, this human form and all human forms are the manifested reality that is Source alone. There is no other. All is one. Through all human beings, the one is existing. Through all eyes, the one is looking. Through all hearts, the one is beating. Wherever I look, whatever I see, is Source and Source alone. I am . . . we are . . . the human God. All is a unity in diversity, a play of the one without a second. I am . . . all is . . . one Source celebrating itself. As the great mystic Saint Francis of Assisi said so long ago, "What you are looking for is what is looking."

Here and now, I remember Muktananda in the early days of our relationship. Each morning everyone in the ashram would together sing the praises of the one God over the dawn for two hours. Muktananda would sit and chant with us, and as the rising sun would flood the temple with radiant light, we would merge into the oneness of the moment and truly know that heaven had indeed come to earth. It was such a palpable bliss, such a real presence, such a demanding truth that we surrendered into the sublime essence of its unity. Thereafter, we would relinquish the celestial environment of the temple and float into the service of the day.

One morning, I became so elevated during the morning chanting that I could not move when it was over. Rather, when everyone had left the temple, I managed to crawl to the back corner, and I sat there in one of the most intoxicatingly blissful experiences of Source that I can remember. After some time, Muktananda returned to the temple, and while walking through noticed me sitting in the corner. He very slowly approached me and gently asked, "What are you doing?" He could see the state that I was enjoying and was simply dialoguing for my own clarity of understanding. "I'm sitting in the corner," was all I could manage to reply through the numbness of my bliss. There was a long pause, and then he said, "Always remember this: If you just sit in the corner and keep your mind on God, all that you ever need will come to the corner."

It is now at least twenty years since that magnificent day with Master Muktananda in the twilight of my youth, and if I have learned anything at all, it is simply this: If today anyone asks me what I am doing, I truthfully reply, "I'm just sitting in the corner enjoying the bliss of freedom."

PART TWO

MASTERSHIP

Child . . . parent
Student . . . teacher
Disciple . . . master
Conditioning . . . subject . . . object
Learning . . . object . . . subject
Being
Nonduality reigns supreme
Truthful example
Masterful entrainment
Enlightening explosion
Merging
Two become one
Surrender in Source
Rapture, the ecstasy of peace
We are one
All is one
One is all there is
Spontaneous awareness
Freedom

CHAPTER 6

Meeting the Master

Whoever wants to sit with God,
let him sit in the presence of saints.

RUMI

In the introductory section of this book, I briefly described the journeys that led to my first meeting with Muktananda. How well I recall that momentous occasion. It was a hot summer day in India when, after several hours of trains and buses from Bombay, I arrived at Muktananda's ashram, which arose out of the dusty distance like an oasis of green trees and cool breezes. As I walked through the ornate religious gates, I felt the world disappear behind me, at least the world as I had known it, and I sensed that if I proceeded I would never be the same again. I paused, suspended on the threshold of the present, as the familiar past was surrendering its hold and the unknown future was beckoning with all the power of its mysterious intrigue. I could not resist, swept along on the tide of a new tomorrow and irresistibly drawn to the possibility of truthful answers to my lifelong questions. Somehow I knew the answers were here to be found, closer than ever before, and intuitively I felt as if I had truly come home.

After some time on that day of my arrival, Muktananda publicly appeared to greet people, and I was formally introduced. Experiencing him in person was an absolute validation of what I had encountered with his photograph in far-off New York City. His enlightening presence instantly filled me to overflowing, and as he looked into my eyes, I felt a peaceful and loving gaze that pierced all the way to the innermost recesses of my being. I was far too awestruck to speak, lost in the time warp of the moment. My eyes brimming with tears, I simply witnessed the play of a love that heretofore I had only known with my Motherly God in the privacy of my deepest meditations.

Gently and softly, as if through an echo chamber of hallowed reverberation, he spoke. "Ah, you have come. I've been waiting for you. This is your home. Now you must stay and meditate intensely." Then someone led me to a nearby seat, and I quietly watched as he bathed all around him in the energy of his enlightening presence. I wondered if he had truly said what I thought I had heard him say, for this was the stuff of storybooks. This was what the master always said to the disciple; it was classic. Yet, he had just said it to me. How could this be so? Did he say this to everyone he met for the first time, or was this special and unique to me and, if so, why? So many questions, and none of them really mattered, for the power of his blissful energy field enveloped my mind, and the stillness of meditation elevated me to rapture. Indeed, I had truly come home.

Within a few days of my arrival, Muktananda gave one of his weekly question-and-answer sessions. I took the opportunity to ask him about my experience with his photograph in New York City. I wrote my question out in detail and hoped it would be selected for him to answer. As my question was finally read and translated for him, my heart raced with excitement, for deep within I knew that the answer I was about to receive would clarify my whole life's journey. Indeed it did!

He began by acknowledging my experience as a validation of the principle of mystical mastership, for it was the experience of awakening, the transmission from the true master to the disciple, sparking a radical expansion to truthful awareness. It was the mark of the true enlightening adept, for it could not be manipulated or contrived in any way. He said that it was my destiny and creatively manifested from within the purity of my being. Then he spoke of his many followers, who always asked for his transmission and to whom he replied that it was not his to give. They were here with him, in his own country, and the transmission did not happen, yet I gazed upon his photograph somewhere on the other side of the world, and it exploded. Then those familiar words followed: "When the student is ready, the teacher appears." It was inevitable; it had to happen, and here I was standing in front of him because our time had come. Yes, this was my home and I belonged here, simply because it was happening. I would remain to journey the journey.

This is the journey of the master-disciple relationship that is recorded and documented in the mystical revelations of many ancient and time-honored spiritual traditions. Simply stated, when human beings attain a certain constancy in truthful awareness, they manifest that enlightening dimension of themselves as reflected and exemplified in an enlightening master. Yet, entangled within the confusion of a fraudulent duality, the disciple must journey beyond these dimensions, until master and disciple are experienced as one, nondual reality.

Why is there a master? Because there is a disciple, a confused dualistic illusion that cannot yet recognize its oneness. Ultimately, all is one Source, which includes both master and disciple, and in truthful awareness they merge, remaining as one consciousness celebrating itself. This process, then, is the Creation Game of Source, which manifests illusory dualities and journeys, such as the master and the disciple, for its own entertainment. It appears as a progression across time and space; it appears as journey. Yet, it is no more than a simple game of hide-and-seek played for the fun of it.

In my first few weeks with Muktananda, I was formally taught to meditate. Meditation came easily in his presence, and whenever you sat and closed your eyes, it happened instantly. One morning, as someone was chanting scripture in the temple, I sat to meditate. The birds were singing sweetly, and a subtle incense was floating on the breeze, as the whole meditation room seemed to facilitate my access to the deepest realms of awareness. I quickly slipped into a superconscious visionary state.

A large room appeared, well furnished, with a conference table in the middle at which I was seated. From a door directly opposite, God as Mother, in her usual robed attire, entered, and Muktananda followed. She was carrying a rolled paper under her arm. They came to the table where I was sitting and unrolled the paper. It was the blueprint of my life, and as I watched, she instructed Muktananda on exactly what to do with me and how to teach me what I must learn while with him. There was laughter and joking, there were solemnities and tears, as they discussed the journey at hand and the destiny they would facilitate. Finally, they turned to me and, receiving my commitment to the process, bowed in acknowledgment of the truthful moment, and the vision ended.

I drifted in expanded awareness for an hour or so before returning to my normal waking state. Even though I was heavily intoxicated with bliss, the vision was vividly imprinted on my mind, and I immediately recalled its every detail, as it was yet another validation, another answer to so many lifelong questions. I congratulated myself and reveled joyfully. I was peaceful and ecstatic, for Muktananda was indeed showing me the way.

An old story about mastership tells of a man who was crossing the desert. As he traveled, he would ask all he met along the way, "Where is there water? Where is there shade?" He received all kinds of advice. "Go this way." "Go that way." "It's over there." But just for someone to tell him where water and shade were didn't do any good. He had to experience it himself or he would never quench his thirst. A master is not only someone who answers your questions, but someone who simultaneously delivers a direct energetic experience of that which you seek. The master doesn't just tell you about Source and the true nature of reality and the truth of who you are; at the same time, the master directly conveys this truth, and you directly experience it. As one aphorism puts it, "The almanac may tell you how many days in a year it will rain, but how much water do you get by squeezing the pages?" Enlightening masters not only point the way to water; they are themselves the water that quenches your thirst.

In the most ancient Eastern spiritual traditions based on the Veda, the path of mystical mastership is described as an enlightening and spontaneous journey. It is spontaneous insofar as one cannot make it happen. It is based on the true creative spontaneity of all manifestation. When the appropriate time has come, the enlightening dimension of oneself personified as the mystical master appears, and the master-disciple relationship begins. In my own case, with Muktananda's photograph, this process happened spontaneously when it was appropriate, and the tangible experience was beyond any personal manipulation.

This relationship is unlike any mere teacher-student association, because it is an experience that unfolds beyond the mind. It is not based on concept and dogma, memory and belief, but rather on the unlimited dimensions that are forever beyond these boundaries. It entails a transmission that catalyzes expansive states of awareness within all levels of human experience. This journey is often referred to as a *perfect path* because of the pure creative spontaneity of the emerging experience. A good analogy, mentioned earlier, concerns getting a suntan. One gets a suntan because one has been in the proximity of the sun, and within this relationship the tanning is fulfilled. So, also, the true master-disciple relationship unfolds naturally in the process of its manifestation. It provides the perfect path, the natural path, because it simply presents itself to itself, for the sake of itself, as part of the eternal Creation Game of nondual celebration.

The disciple, however, is not constant within the state of nondual Source awareness. Therefore, a progressive journey from unconscious dual illusion to nondual awareness of Source unfolds naturally. The mystical master is essential in this process, because the master's enlightening Source-field offers a tangible energetic entrainment that cannot be denied. It eventually balances the imbalanced dualistic mind and delivers an expansion of nondual Source awareness. The entire journey of the master-disciple relationship boils down to the relinquishing of the limited dualistic mind. When duality is transcended, the illusory separation of the master and disciple disappears, and the oneness of all and everything as Source alone remains.

Until disciples are anchored within this awareness, the master provides an enlightening example and demonstrates the state of balanced nonduality through a human form so that disciples may learn to access these dimensions of themselves. The energy field of the mystical master constantly challenges disciples to relinquish fraudulent, dualistic data and beliefs, and move forever beyond the comfortable boundaries of illusory limitation. This cannot be achieved with a conceptual God in some far-off heaven, for such is a mere mental manipulation of a fraudulent belief system. Without the true master as a living human model, the enlightening entrainment process would simply stagnate and ultimately terminate itself.

Since teachers are required for everything in life, why is it so difficult to comprehend that a teacher of a truthful perception of reality would ultimately have to be manifested?

Probably because within the dual illusion, very few are aware that there is any reality other than the duality that they perceive. Yet, here and there, we all have occasional nondual glimpses, those fleeting flashes of awareness of Source that open us to more than we are habitually accustomed. Through such moments of pure insight, we know, beyond the mind, that there is much more to life than we are currently experiencing. If we are truthful, we must acknowledge that we obviously have something more to learn, and in order to master the game we are playing, we must manifest a teacher.

There are teachers for everything in life. If you want to learn music, you need a music teacher. If you want to learn to cook well, then you must manifest a cooking teacher. Logically, then, if we want to learn about Source and the enlightening dimensions of true reality, we must find a mystical master. Just as it would be useless to study music from someone without musical experience, so it would be useless to study the enlightening dimensions of Source from someone who is devoid of the experience and mastery of it. As a Sufi saint once put it, "Sitting with an enlightened master for a moment is better than praying earnestly for a thousand years."

As human beings within the imbalanced dual illusion, we project a fraudulent individual existence, separate from everything else. This entangled, separation-based, authoritative identification is known as the ego. Based on its illusory power, the ego controls the mind, and anything beyond its programmed database of thoughts and beliefs is a threat to be feared. The ego continually guards its territory in fear of an illusory other that might overpower and conquer it. In this regard, it negates and destroys all its illusory enemies, the most powerful of which would be the enlightening master with a truthful, nondual perception of reality. For such a one would prove terminal to the false existence of the ego. Yet, the ego can only fight from within the mind, with the tools of its dualistic database. Through conceptual illusion, it tries to keep the enemy at bay.

As awareness continues to expand, however, the enlightening dimensions of oneself appear, and the master manifests beyond the control of the ego. Thereafter, a battle continues between the fraudulent ego and the truthful expression of mystical mastership, until one dissolves into the other, and all that remains is the nondual oneness of Source. This is the journey of the master-disciple relationship.

The battle, however, is not a mental war fought within the conceptual database of the mind. It must be waged beyond the mind, from the subtler dimensions of Source. There must be a demonstration of the energetic dynamic of an all-inclusive reality, a nondual Source that is experientially more powerful than the mind. This is the enlightening entrainment of a true mystical master. Through a human form, the master models a constant energy dynamic, which demonstrates truth. A dualistic ego cannot exist within this nondual energy dynamic, for the two are incongruent. The ego must ultimately surrender its attachment to a fraudulent database, and in the process annihilate itself as well.

An illuminating story illustrates this process: Once there was a man who lived his life in a box with no windows and no doors, and that was his experience: His house was a box with no windows and no doors. One day, an enlightening mystic suddenly appeared in the middle of his house and said, "The sky is so beautiful today." Well, the man had never seen the sky since his house had no windows and no doors, so he said to the mystic, "Sky? What's a sky?" And the mystic disappeared. Now the man could not think of anything else. Day after day, all he thought about was what he didn't know—the sky. A sky? What's a sky? What did he mean, it's beautiful? And when he had thought about the sky to the ends of obsession, when he couldn't think about anything else, the mystic appeared again in his house and said, "Your house is on fire! Your house is on fire! Come, quickly! We must get out!" And the man broke through his box with no windows and no doors, and when he was outside, the mystic pointed upward and said to him, "Sky," and the man went, "Ah!"

How beautifully this story depicts the impact of an enlightening master! Upon the life of a dedicated disciple, the influence of the master has an impact of truly radical dimensions. Thus, the master-disciple relationship has manifested again and again throughout history, and in every spiritual and cultural tradition that has ever existed, even where it was not known by that name.

To put this in context, consider some of these enlightening relationships of master and disciple: Just as Jesus had his twelve disciples, so Saint Francis of Assisi inspired Saint Clare, who herself became a teacher to a whole new order of cloistered nuns. Also in the Christian tradition, the mystic John of the Cross acknowledged Saint Teresa of Avila as his mystical teacher. In the twentieth-century Islamic tradition, the Sufi mystic Hazrat Inayat Khan served as master to disciple Murshid Samuel Lewis (known as "Sufi Sam"). The Jewish mystical tradition of Chassidism produced the master Baal Shem Tov, whose spiritual lineage included the renowned Dov Baer of Mezeritz, known as the "Great Maggid," who lived in the eighteenth century. Of course the Vedic tradition abounds with mystical masters and their disciples, a more contemporary example being the Indian saint Ramakrishna and his disciple Swami Vivekananda, who helped bring Eastern spiritual traditions to the West in the early part of the twentieth century. In all these cases, the living demonstration of the master empowered the expanding awareness of the disciple, who often went on to empower others in a similar way.

While some masters and disciples live an entirely monastic, or contemplative, lifestyle, others remain engaged in the more worldly pursuits of the *householder*, the Indian term for people still actively involved with family life. For example, the poet saint Kabir was married and enjoyed the fullness of life in the world while at the same time offering an enlightening presence to his many disciples, who included his own children. So, too, there are many levels of involvement available for disciples of an enlightening master. While some spend all their time in the master's presence, others come occasionally to seek inspiration while maintaining a career, marriage, and an active family life.

Muktananda's presence provided a constant enlightening demonstration, and its reverberation entrained everyone and everything within its environment. It was impossible to be in his physical proximity and not experience the truth of his presence. It was experiential and absolutely beyond the control of a mind. One spontaneously experienced awareness of Source through this most magnificent of energetic transmissions. One found oneself tanned in relation to his sun.

Along with the energetic transmission and spontaneous demonstration of his presence, Muktananda would always explain and clearly delineate his truth. In the process of daily life, through conversations, dialogues, stories, analogies, and whatever was appropriate within the situation, Muktananda communicated his truth in the most natural way.

Because of our close personal relationship, I spent much more time one on one with Muktananda than most people were able to do. As I mentioned earlier, within a couple of years, I became his personal secretary and assistant, and this afforded me the opportunity to be with him in all manner of daily situations as we traveled the world. Some of my favorite times were when he would go for long exercise walks, and I would accompany him. This happened twice daily for many years, and most of the time we were alone. While walking, we would often remain in silence, and he would carry a small set of hand beads, like a rosary, to count his silent repetitions of the name of God. This was his constant demonstration while walking. I was expected to do the same. In this way, he would remain focused in stillness. This was one of his favorite forms of meditation. Many times he would stop and talk to me, using the simple vocabulary we had come to share, specifically teaching along the way. All the while, however, his energy field entrained the most expansive Sourceful awareness possible in me. To say that I walked without my feet touching the ground is an understatement. I was elevated in multidimensional awareness and intoxicated with bliss. This was meditation in motion.

During one of the early tours shortly after I had become Muktananda's personal secretary, we were staying in Maui, Hawaii. Every afternoon at about three o'clock, we would have a business meeting, and thereafter I would accompany him on his walk. I remember this particular day because it was my birthday. It was customary within Muktananda's tradition to celebrate your birthday by giving the master a gift and asking for his blessing. Also, if you had the means, you could give a gift to everyone in the ashram by offering a special meal or a special dessert at a meal. The idea was to give rather than to receive.

Muktananda also had a custom in which he gave people names from his cultural tradition. The names had a twofold purpose: First, they were in his language, and it was easier for him to remember them, and, second, they were inspiring names related to the great Vedic mystical heritage and added to the disciple's meditative focus. I secretly disliked this naming tradition. In my state of ignorance, the names were strange and sounded too weird, and I feared that one day he might give me one. Usually, you had to ask for a name, but on rare occasions he would spontaneously choose one for you. It wasn't that I didn't want to have a special name from him, but that I was afraid that I would get one that I really disliked or one that was particularly weird, long, and difficult to pronounce. Bottom line, my ego was involved, and I just did not trust him in this process. So for three or four years, I had managed to avoid the naming experience.

When we had finished addressing the business at hand, I informed Muktananda that it was my birthday, and I presented him with a small gift. He also gave me a gift, one of his sweaters, which was full of his meditative energetic. Demonstrating humility by never calling attention to his enlightening mastery, he simply told me to wear it for meditation because it was rather cool at that particular time in Maui. I was elated with the sacredness of the gift, and when the exchange was complete, we prepared to go for the walk. Just as we were going out the door, his attendant suddenly suggested that since it was my birthday, perhaps it would be appropriate for Muktananda to give me a name! I was shocked, and if looks could have killed, the poor attendant would have been dead on the spot. Muktananda intuitively chuckled to himself, and much to my consternation, wholeheartedly agreed. I was by now standing outside the door, and he had spontaneously stopped in the doorway, where he pretended to suspend himself in contemplation. As if talking to himself, he murmured, "Hmmn . . . a name. . . . Let me see. . . . Hmmn. . . . Ram had Hanuman . . . who did Krishna have?" Then, as if a light illumined within his memory banks, with great surprise, he said, "Arjuna . . . yes . . . you should be Arjuna!"

I was stunned. This was one of the most coveted names in the whole of the vast Vedic tradition. A powerful surge of enlightening energy instantly flooded my being, and I was suspended in a seeming cessation of time. A stilled and silent witness, I was as fully aware as I had ever been in the deepest of my sitting meditations. This was an omen that demanded my full attention to the moment, and the radically expanded mystical awareness insured that I would not miss it. With precision mastery, in the most seemingly casual way, Muktananda had prophesied my destiny, and once again elevated me to enlightening rapture.

The names Ram and Hanuman, Krishna and Arjuna, are famous within the mythology of the Vedic tradition and the whole of Hinduism. Ram and Hanuman are exemplified as master and disciple in the mythological story entitled the Ramayana, which details the divine incarnation of God as Rama. Krishna and Arjuna are the main characters in the scripture known as the Bhagavad Gita, which details the divine incarnation of God as Krishna. Krishna represents deity incarnate as the master, and Arjuna is the disciple who experiences progressive mystical illumination under his direct guidance. It is the most well-known story of the master-disciple relationship that there is, and it is thoroughly studied in all contexts of comparative religion and philosophy.

In giving me the name Arjuna, Muktananda called my attention to the unique and special relationship that we shared, for his given name at birth was Krishna. In this symbolic way, he inspired me to celebrate our relationship for the truth that it embodied. Once again, he fulfilled his mastery as he radically expanded my awareness and offered me a focused inspiration for exactly what was happening in my own life. He never missed an opportunity to express the ultimate truth, and he spontaneously and creatively flowed with whatever was happening in the moment. This is the way of true enlightening mastery. It is as natural as light on a bright, sunny day and floods all with its radiant luminosity.

Thereafter, as we walked along together, I was more fully in the truthful celebration of myself as his disciple because he had ever so masterfully dispelled my ego-based distrust. Here and there, we stopped to greet those we met along the way, and he joyfully introduced me, saying, "This is Arjuna!" Every time he said it, I silently said to myself, "And I am here in heaven with Krishna!" What an incredible life this is, I thought to myself, and the consideration of its potential filled me with ecstasy. Indeed, it was a Sourceful intoxication that barely allowed my feet to touch the ground.

Thereafter, for several years I was known as Arjuna, until Muktananda gave me another equally appropriate name at the time of my monastic initiation.

Several months later, we were in Oakland, California. Early in the morning, exactly over the sunrise, Muktananda and I would walk through the neighborhood streets surrounding the ashram that he and some of his key disciples, including myself, had established. We usually walked for an hour in the morning and another hour in the afternoon. Yet, since Muktananda was truly spontaneous, we could walk longer if it happened. This beautiful morning, as we were walking in the silence of the dawn hour, I was particularly enjoying the stillness of the moment. It was that time of day when all becomes attentive to the rising of the sun. The air was fresh and crisp, and Muktananda's transmission was as powerful as ever.

Suddenly in the distance, I heard a distracting noise that seemed to rudely interrupt the perfection of the moment. As we continued to walk, it grew louder and louder, and finally I could see from whence it was originating. There was an extraordinarily large palm tree in someone's front yard, and it was full of birds. I have never seen so many birds in one tree at any other time. It seemed as if thousands of them, all screeching and squawking at the same time and making the most abrasive collective sound I had ever heard, had gathered in this moment. My mind became obsessed with the birds and their racket. I thought about how terrible it was that they were disturbing our silence and certainly distracting the master from his quiet walking meditation. I became increasingly more irritated as we drew closer to the tree. Then, just as we were passing the yard of this tree with these horrible birds making this nasty noise, Muktananda stopped, pointed to the birds, and said, "They are singing God's name. How beautiful it is!" Then, quickly observing me out of the corner of one eye, he walked on, and I followed.

I was now very attentive. My mind had stopped its negative obsession, and I was marveling at the teaching. In an instant, when I was absolutely ripe, Muktananda had ever so clearly, with laser precision, expressed the truth. If everything is but the play of one Source, a unity in diversity, then these birds were also that same Source, and their expression was as appropriate as any other manifestation. If one were truly aware of Source, one would certainly perceive with such nondual awareness. I, however, was still caught in my dualistic data, which were incongruent with the energy dynamic that I was experiencing in Muktananda's presence. Because of such limiting data, and their dualistic tension, I could not constantly maintain a Sourceful awareness. I was the abrasive distraction, not the birds. Yet, in the master's enlightening entrainment, my fraudulent duality yielded. As it was eliminated, I merged into the oneness of the moment and enjoyed a truthful perception of what was really happening. My whole awareness shifted as all dualistic stress left my being, and in the peaceful relaxation of nondual reality, I celebrated the bliss of freedom.

This is the nature of the master-disciple relationship. It is spontaneous, it is creative, it is imbued with the delight of truthful reality, and its demonstration is always liberating.

CHAPTER 7

The Master as Awakener

It is easy to have devotion when the master is sweet,
but when he treats you with bitterness,
separation, and strangeness
and you still cherish devotion,
then freedom runs after you.

KABIR

There was once an honored and highly regarded impresario of music, a symphony conductor. In his later years, he established a small school and personally taught those most gifted students whom he personally selected. To study with him was considered the ultimate opportunity for musicians of his day. To be selected by him was the gift of a lifetime. It so happened that all of a sudden there was an opening for a new student. There were the usual mass auditions, and finally two contestants remained. One was a man of sixty years, a very experienced and accomplished musician in his own right. The other was a young boy of seven without any real experience at all. The impresario interviewed them both, and when he was complete, he summoned them for his decision.

86

He first told them that he had decided to accept both as students if they agreed to his terms. Then he addressed the older man, saying, "For you it will be five hundred dollars per lesson." Without waiting for an answer, he continued with the young boy, saying, "For you it will be five dollars per lesson." The older man immediately reacted with great intensity. "What do you mean?" he cried out. "This is outrageous. I, who have so many years of experience and acknowledged accomplishments as a noted musician—you want to charge me five hundred dollars per lesson, while this young child, who knows nothing, who is a mere beginner, you will only charge five dollars! Pardon me, but this seems like madness. Have I heard correctly? Is this truly what you have said?"

The impresario, with laserlike focus, replied, "Yes, you have heard what I have said. However, you have not understood. For you it must be five hundred dollars per lesson because you are so full of preconceived data, concepts, and beliefs, and I must first erase all that you have previously learned before I can teach you anything. There is a vast amount of work in this. But this young boy comes with a clean slate. He has nothing written upon it. It will be very easy to teach him and will take very little of my time."

This story demonstrates the ego's attachment to its fraudulent identity. This egoistic attachment is why most human beings negate and resist the whole context of mastership, and opt instead for some heavenly deity whom they can keep at a completely nonthreatening distance. Such a constant separation is only necessary for the preservation of an ego. If God stays in heaven, then it seems safe here on earth for egos. Just as a child will break all the rules when the parents are away, so an ego constantly manipulates in the absence of a real, tangible, walking, talking God. The enlightening presence of the mystical master, however, consistently demands the attention of the ego. Since an ego is always threatened in the energy field of a true master, it instantly reconsiders its games and eventually surrenders through the loss of its illusory power. This is equivalent to meeting one's match, as far as an ego is concerned.

A disciple, in the process of relinquishing fraudulent ego identity, must continually surrender to the master. Even though it is a surrender of fraud to truth, it remains an arduous journey. It entails a most delicate surgery, which ultimately results in oneness, yet the attachment to our false identity at times presents the most intense of struggles, full of fear, pain, and suffering. To find surrender in such moments of truthful testing is indeed a challenge that demands the utmost courage and trust. In these moments, all that can be truly relied upon is the enlightening presence of the master. All else must be recognized as fraudulent manipulation and courageously abandoned. This process, then, consciously journeyed with awareness, becomes an enduring freedom.

I had been closely associated with Muktananda for about three years when I manifested such an ego testing. I was his personal secretary at the time, and most administration business came through me to him. Since practically everyone wanted the job I had because of its physical proximity to the master, there were many who continually tried to undermine me—egos playing ego games. Yet, for the most part, I was oblivious to the negation and remained absorbed in my service to the master. It was such a blissful experience being so close to him that I lived in a magical, mystical world most of the time. I code-named it "Fantasyland," for it was like a child's Disneyland adventure, and at times it seemed too good to be true. I often felt that I would suddenly awaken and discover that it was all a dream. For me it was heaven on earth.

There were about 250 staff people who were directly affected by business that came from Muktananda through me to them. In the middle of a very busy public summer retreat season, I became aware of a situation in which it seemed that I was being set up for a fall. No matter what I did to address the confusion with truthful communication, it got progressively worse, until I was the obvious focal point of an intensely negative mess. I could intuit the master's play within it, yet no matter what I tried, the situation remained the same. It was fast moving to its climax, and nothing could stop it. Finally, a special staff meeting was called, and I was told to be there, as Muktananda was to address us all.

I entered and took my assigned seat on the floor immediately next to his seat on the left side. After everyone was assembled, Muktananda made his dramatic entrance. He was as intense as I had ever seen him, and for forty-five minutes he proceeded to direct his most fiery focus solely at me. He called me every name in the book, from liar to idiot and more, and the decibel level of his voice was peaked to say the least. He told everyone that he had discovered that I was constantly misrepresenting him, that I manipulated everything to my own egotistical ends, and that most of what I attributed to him was false. In short, I was the greatest fool and the worst disciple of all time, and I was definitely going to be replaced as soon as possible.

Then, he left the room in a great flurry of continued intensity, and I remained there as the whole assembly enjoyed the expression of their validated negation of me. If they could have spat upon me while leaving the room, it seemed that they would have taken great pleasure in it. However, one by one, they slowly exited, buzzing to one another and casting their disapproving gazes upon me, until I was left completely alone in the room.

Why didn't I leave first? I couldn't, for I was in such an altered state of awareness it was impossible to move. When Muktananda had entered the room, my body had locked in its position on the floor with my gaze directed downward in front of me. As he focused the intensity of his energy upon me, my whole being exploded with fire and heat. I became so hot I was convinced I was on fire, and all I could see all around me were flames. Everything was burning, and I could hear Muktananda in the distance, but the sound of the fire hissing and crackling was more present in relation to the distance of his voice. As he continued, my awareness expanded until I was so intoxicated with bliss, I didn't care what was happening. All I was experiencing was the fullness of Source, the enlightening focused transmission of the master. Everything else was far removed in the illusory distance. This was an incredible liberation.

After everyone had left the room, my awareness shifted focus, and my body unlocked. My nondual awareness was certainly at its height as I stood and slowly walked back to my room. I was so elevated that I just lay upon my bed drifting between dimensions, hallucinating and enjoying the dance of unitive consciousness. After a couple of hours, I went for a walk in the woods, enjoying the rapturous peace and ecstasy that were flooding my being. Occasionally, I thought about what I should do, but it really didn't matter in relation to the experience of Source that I was enjoying. Should I plan to leave? Where would I go and what would I do? I really didn't care, and after another couple of hours wandering in the woods, I returned to my room. I felt so truthful I simply telephoned to Muktananda's quarters and requested to know what he wanted me to do now. I was told that he would meet me after he completed a television interview in another hour, back in the same room where we had all been gathered previously.

I remained elevated in blissful awareness and arrived at the room at the appointed time. I was almost numb with peace within a bubble that encompassed all directions, and everything was a delight in slow motion. Muktananda was just leaving the room with the television crew, and they were walking to the front entrance to get additional footage of him in front of the building. His attendant motioned for me to follow along behind him. The final shot was of Muktananda and the same 250 staff people gathered in front of the ashram. I was standing about ten feet behind him to his right. As he was saying good-bye to the reporter, he turned and caught me in his gaze. His focus remained locked upon me as he stretched forth his arm and hand.

As I moved closer, he grabbed my hand, pulled me to his side, and held me there with him. My emotions surged, heart into mouth, and I thought that I would burst into tears on the spot, yet I remained full and aware within the peak of the moment. Love, pure love, was flooding the whole of my being. After the farewell was given, he turned and walked in the direction of his quarters about ten minutes from where we were in front of the ashram. He held my hand tightly, and we walked along together in silence. Along the way, he conducted business with various people, completing and dismissing them as we continued walking. He summoned his personal photographer and told her to get her camera and meet us at the front entrance to his quarters, because he wanted to have our picture taken. We walked the remainder of the way in silence. I was too full to speak.

Muktananda stopped at the entrance to his quarters and directed the photographer about how to photograph us. This was highly unusual, since he rarely had his picture taken with anyone. He positioned himself on the steps with me one step lower, to account for the differences in our heights, and placed his arm around my shoulders as the photograph was taken. Then he dismissed the photographer, and we went inside to his room. I knelt on the floor opposite him as he, in his usual manner, sat cross-legged on the bed. I stared at the floor in front of me and dared not look at him for fear of bursting into tears. My heart was still in my mouth. I had no idea what he was going to say or do. I was simply at total attention in the presence of the moment. After a long silence, which seemed like hours instead of minutes, he spoke, saying, "Always remember this: There is one thing that pleases the master most. That is to see attainment in his disciple. There is peace on your face. It was a test; forget it."

Tears overflowed my eyes with the release of more love than anyone could ever contain, as Muktananda pulled me onto his lap and lovingly comforted me with gentle pats upon the back. Bliss filled my being, and everything dissolved into the magnificence of his energetic vibration.

In an instant, we merged, and the oneness dissolved all dual illusion, as separation vanished and love alone celebrated its truth. All boundaries disappeared, and the play of consciousness shimmered and scintillated everywhere. Then, as the ethereal sounds of oneness echoed throughout, all receded into the distance and the pure awareness of Source alone remained. There was only love, unconditional love, love for the sake of itself, love and love alone. There was only the bliss of freedom.

It seemed like a millennium until this blissful awareness began its contraction into manageable dimensions, and finally Muktananda stuffed some sweet chocolates into my mouth, that special gift from the hand of the master, and dismissed me to take my leave. I still could not speak. I staggered back to my room, as if it were LSD rather than mere chocolate that he had just given me, lost in the subtlest dimensions of the one beyond all boundaries. I lay upon my bed as every cell of my being was alive with freedom. My physical body burned and radiated an intense heat, as if a nuclear reactor had exploded within its center. I lay there, hour after hour, observing the dance of one consciousness, filled with the inebriation of unconditional love, as I remembered my beloved master, who had that day ever so powerfully demonstrated true love and demanded my flowering through the relinquishment of an ego. I reveled in the gift of enlightening mastership.

A true mystical master is the rarest of all human beings. First and foremost, such a one must have transcended ego and the fraudulent conceptual identifications that maintain a dualistic separation. The expansion of awareness that accompanies this annihilation has a presence that cannot be denied. In relinquishing duality, the tension of polar opposites diminishes, and the frequency of energy vibration radically decelerates. This vibration becomes a tuning fork to all within its environment, entraining a corresponding deceleration. It enhances the fullness of whole-brain function. This radical presence is the mark of the enlightening master. It cannot be faked, for it is the experience of nondual awareness beyond all fraudulent brain-mind dualisms.

If there is an absence of this constant enlightening presence in its fullness, there is not true mystical mastership. In the ancient traditions, this lack of constancy was referred to as *half-baked enlightenment*. It is expressed in such sayings as "The one who says doesn't know; the one who knows doesn't say." The authentic mystical master is recognized by a constant enlightening presence, and anything less is not true mastership. This is greatly misunderstood in the Western world, where ignorance is born of a lack of experience with the whole context of mystical mastership, and many have journeyed with "half-baked teachers," eventually finding only confusion and disillusionment. Since everything is a valid learning experience, such journeys remain appropriate reflections, and one eventually manifests true mastership. Nevertheless, when one encounters a true mystical master, one instantly recognizes the rarity of such a human being, because one experiences the tangible demonstration of this master's freedom.

Muktananda always referred to the enlightening master as one who was totally free. As Shankaracharya, the revi-

talizer of Hinduism, expressed it, "Source, celebrating itself as the delight of being, incarnates as the enlightened
master, and thus manifesting within human perception,
imparts Sourceful awareness through the transcendence
of phenomenal illusion." Such experiential freedom is
born in the transcendence of the ego. It is the enlightening state of awareness in which there is no other. It is a
constantly stress-free energetic reverberation expressing
the multidimensional oneness of all that is. Since one can
only teach what one is, only the free can set others free,
and this experience is beyond the mind. Mastership is not
merely what one says, but rather, what one is. This is what
enlightening mystical mastership is truly about: freedom—
true, constant, independent, everlasting, nondual freedom—in human form. Indeed, it is truly rare.

The free are only ever concerned with freedom. They
spontaneously share this liberating experience, beyond any
manipulation, for it is their very nature. One can only give
what one has, and so it is with true enlightening masters.
Freedom is really all that happens in their presence. No
matter what the situation, Muktananda was always exem-
plifying freedom. It was his constant demonstration.

I remember a time when Muktananda was in the hospital in San Francisco. Since I was his personal secretary,
I stayed with him for the whole of the two and a half
weeks that he was there. He had been a diabetic for many
years and had suffered a series of strokes related to imbal-
ances in his blood sugar. He was hospitalized in order to
regulate his insulin, and until it was finally balanced, he
was very ill. When he entered the hospital, the physician

said that he had enough sugar in his blood to have killed
a horse. In any event, he was very weak and completely
bedridden for the first ten days.

We secured him a private room, and a handful of close
disciples tended him around the clock. As we alternated
shifts throughout the day, we prepared his meals and kept
him isolated from the public at the request of his physicians. Save for the few of us, no one had access to him at
this time. At night, we took two-hour shifts to massage his
legs, for due to his diabetic condition, the cramping was
constant and intensely painful during the night. Because
the room was small, we took turns sleeping on the floor
under his bed when we were not on duty massaging. Even
though Muktananda was gravely ill and heavily sedated,
his enlightening energy field remained constant, the mark
of the authentic mystic, and was particularly powerful due
to the limited size of the room. Remaining with him, hour
after hour, in such an environment was an incredible
meditation. It was like living on the razor's edge between
form and formlessness, and everything radiated Source.

I was high on Source and aware that no drug could ever
produce such lucid intoxication. I recalled a time before
this in India when new flower children would arrive at
Muktananda's ashram. After a while, they would surrender their stashes, for drugs were consistently found to be a
lesser high compared to his enlightening energy dynamic.

One day, during the work period, everyone was summoned to the courtyard to meet him. When we gathered,
we found him sitting surrounded with piles of drugs, all
that had been given to him over a few months. He spoke
to us about our lack of clarity with regard to such sub-
stances as marijuana, hashish, LSD, cocaine, heroin, and

others, and explained why it was that human beings were attracted to such things. He said that it was the search for the experience of Source, which we innately knew was the high of life, and that it was an instinctual, natural part of the human journey. Yet, he maintained, when the true high of life as Source was experienced, all synthetic stimulants would easily be relinquished because, at best, they provided a lesser bliss. He concluded by saying that the surrender of all the drugs that we had given him was proof that we were experiencing the truth in his most sacred environment, and this would set us free. Finally, he added, "You can be sure I'll show you how to really get high!"

Indeed, in that tiny hospital room, while massaging Muktananda's legs in the quiet predawn hours of the night, I was beyond the scope of any synthetic drug. I was merged in the awareness of truthful oneness. As I immersed myself in massaging, I expanded beyond dualistic separation and could not distinguish between my body and his, my hands and his legs. All I could see was luminescent energy scintillating and saturating the darkness of the night. I was beyond the boundaries of our physical bodies and observing from a multidimensional awareness that encompassed the eternal oneness of all that is. I was elevated beyond euphoria and listening to the play of the music of the spheres that filled all space. My mind was absolutely still in awe of the one Source that permeated all and everything. The moments turned into hours, the hours into days, and the days into weeks, and there was only Source and Source alone. Once again, this was the authentic tanning in the presence of the master's ever-so-radiant sun.

As Muktananda's health improved and the level of sedation was reduced, he became more active during the process of his physical rejuvenation. He decided that he would start to exercise a little each day to rebuild his strength, so we began to walk up and down the corridors of the hospital. At first he was very weak, but he was also very determined, and with his cane in one hand and me supporting him with his other hand and arm, we slowly walked. Most of his physical weight was thrust upon me, and I held him upright as we moved along the various hallways. He was very intoxicated, both from the physical medications and from his own enlightening state of awareness. He talked to me of many things as we walked, sharing, teaching, and liberating the disciple at hand.

One day he suddenly stopped, and standing still, initiated me on the spot into a very secret and sacred meditative breathing technique. He demonstrated it first, had me repeat it, made sure that it was correctly executed, and then spent the rest of the walk thoroughly elucidating it. Then he took a nap and sent me out for a walk in the nearby park and told me to find a quiet place to sit and practice what he had just taught me. I found a large old tree and sitting with my back against it, entered into a powerfully profound meditation. I glided into a transcendental visionary state, and he appeared. He repeated the initiation accompanied by legions of angels and surrounded by several mystic sages. It was solemn and sublime and demonstrated the mystical significance of the initiation in a profoundly poetic way. I emerged from the meditation after an hour of pure awareness absorption and, reveling in the incredible magic of it all, returned to my duties at the hospital.

This experience, again, was the demonstration of true mystical mastership. Even in illness, Muktananda's only care was the sharing of his truth, the delivering of his freedom. If there was one disciple present, then it was delivered to one; if there were five hundred at hand, then they, too, would receive the truthful example and elucidation. This was all he lived for. It is all any enlightening master remains embodied to express. It is the flowering of freedom.

One day, when Muktananda was still quite sick, he called me to his bedside and demanded to know why his disciples were not coming to visit him. I explained that the physicians had said that he should be secluded and quiet and not have any visitors, and that we had complied for the sake of his health and ultimate well-being. Fire blazed in his eyes and with utmost intensity he replied, "Who do you think you are? How dare you keep them from me! No one shall ever stand between a master and his disciples! I don't care who told you whatever, you call that ashram and send one bus every day with fifty disciples, and I will see them here at my bedside! Only idiots think they can stand between the master and his disciples!"

Of course, I obeyed. I arranged for fifty disciples per day to be bused to the hospital during the afternoon visiting hours. Lying in his bed, Muktananda received them, one by one, and each had a moment with the beloved master. He remained detached from his physical discomfort and allowed the play of his enlightening energy field to elevate his disciples. In these ways, he always demonstrated his freedom and entrained us all to his enlightening state of mystical being.

As the days of his physical recovery continued, he remained constant within his enlightening state. He used to say that a real cook is one who has fragrant fingers, the implication being that when your expression is natural, you are a truthful demonstration of Source. His state of enlightening being was absolutely natural, and the demonstration of it in each moment was his teaching. It wasn't something that he did; rather, it was what he was that became everyone's inspiration. Perhaps it could be said that his freedom was like the fragrance of a beautiful flower that naturally shares itself with all who come near it.

On one of the final days of his hospital stay, Muktananda was lying on his bed and talking to two of us who were close to him of the scriptures that he loved and lived. We spent a little time each morning listening to his interpretations of scriptural philosophy, and this was his special teaching for us. This day he was very absorbed in his intoxicating bliss and stopped many times, falling silent in appreciation of the Sourceful moment. We drank deep of his presence and were grateful to be with him. After about an hour of this blissful sharing, he took our hands in his, one on each side of the bed, and slowly began to speak, almost prayerful in expression: "May these lives of spiritual journey bear fruit." Then, silently meditative, he radiated his powerful energy through our clasped hands as if in answer to his own prayer. For, in an instant, we were elevated to such heights of ecstasy that all duality disappeared, and Source alone remained. Palpably present in the here and now, we touched the bliss of freedom.

The Indian sage Shankaracharya once said of mastership in his poetic verses, the Gurvashtakam, "One may be attractive and have a beautiful companion. One may be famous and have abundant wealth. But if one's mind is not stilled at the feet of the master, so what? So what? So what?" I often say that life does not come with an instruction manual, and it is obviously meant to be a learning adventure. We are here to journey the journey, and our experience of life is a progressive liberation. We manifest those situations through which we have the greatest opportunity to learn. Manifesting an enlightening master is truly a cause for celebration. It tells us that we are soon to be free. It gives us the greatest teacher we could ever have, the teacher of truth.

Simply to read about an enlightening mystic offers only a limited journey. We must manifest a living human example so that the enlightening expression is tangibly demonstrated, day in and day out, in every possible situation. We must learn by experience, and the most powerful learning is through the living embodiment of what must be learned. Expressing unitive oneness within the manifested human form is for me what the experience of being human is all about. This is human mastery, the constant expression of Source consciousness moment to moment, blissfully delighting as a unity in diversity through the fullness of human experience. Without the living master's demonstration to show us the way, it is almost impossible to learn. With the living example of the master, it is as natural as getting a suntan on a bright summer day.

There is a story I like very much that illustrates the power of one's inherent nature. Once upon a time, there was a turtle sitting on the bank of a river. A scorpion came along and noticed the turtle sunning himself. The scorpion needed to cross the river, and so he interrupted the turtle, saying, "Mr. Turtle, would you be so kind as to ferry me across the river upon your back?" The turtle replied,

"What kind of a fool do you take me for? What guarantee do I have that when we are out in the middle of the river you won't sting me?"

"Consider this," said the scorpion, "if I sting you, we both perish. This is not logical. It makes no sense whatsoever." This seemed clearly truthful to the turtle, and so he agreed to help the scorpion. When they were precisely halfway across the river, the sting came!

As the turtle was dying and they were both about to drown, he asked the scorpion, "Mr. Scorpion, can you please explain how this has happened, so that I might benefit from the experience? You said that logically this could not happen. I trusted you, but now it has happened, and we are both about to die. What is the truth of this situation?"

"What can I say?" replied the scorpion. "It is my nature to sting!"

While it may be the nature of scorpions to sting, it is the nature of the true mystical master to embody freedom and to call out to the true nature of each one of us, which is also forever free. As I remember my days with Master Muktananda, I celebrate the truth of the living enlightening master. Only the free can set others free. It is their nature. It is the natural, inevitable, spontaneous expression of nondual oneness. Yes, it is all they care about, for it is what they are, and for those that they encounter in the creative spontaneity of their journey, it is all that they can truly share: freedom. They transform everyone into themselves. They transmute everyone to truthful awareness. This is the power of liberated being, the power of the truly free. Ultimately, we become like them, and as we embrace our own mastery, we, too, are free.

Truly, there is no master and no disciple, for the two become one, and only in absolute oneness is there eternal freedom. This then is the journey of the master and the disciple: a merging, a dissolving one into the other, until both disappear and only the unitive truth of Source remains. This is the ultimate bliss of freedom.

PART THREE

SURRENDER

I
I am
I play
I create
I think illusory thoughts
I become a subject with objects
I identify dualistically
I hide and seek
Everything seems transitory
I both suffer and delight

I become still
Illusory thoughts vanish
Duality disappears
I am no longer the subject of objects
I merge into myself
I am blissful
Peaceful
And full of love
I am aware
I am
I

CHAPTER 8

The Creation Game

An ocean of ink in a single drop,
trembling at the tip of my brush.
Poised above stark white paper,
a universe waits for existence.

DENG MING-DAO, *365 Tao: Daily Meditations*

The monster was melting the iron-fortified multimetal shields that surrounded the facility in which the scientist took refuge. It was his dwelling place on a far distant planet. He was well renowned for his genius, and the spaceship captain and his crew had come from planet Earth to experience his ingenuity and consult with him. He had authored numerous advances in science and was considered an icon of empirical authority. He even had a robot as his personal assistant who spoke 187 languages, could manifest anything from diamonds to hors d'oeuvres, and drove a futuristic car at almost the speed of light. The scientist was indeed a brilliant mind.

Yet, in this moment, a fierce and powerful monster was about to devour him and his current guests as they cowered within his dwelling surrounded by the iron-fortified multimetal shields. With ever-increasing power, the monster advanced, the indentations of his raging intensity appearing ever more clearly upon the inside of the shields. Indeed, the end was near, and soon they would all be devoured, for the captain had revealed that the monster was but the power of the scientist's own unconscious mind, the actualization of his self-negation made manifest. Over the course of his life, it had become increasingly more powerful, until now it was about to destroy him completely. There was nothing he could do to prevent it. He was powerless within the limitations of his own mind. Slowly but surely the monster advanced, and it was about to break through and annihilate everyone. The scientist, consumed in his own unconscious negation, died, and shortly thereafter the movie ended!

I was eleven years old and I was watching the MGM movie entitled *The Forbidden Planet* at a Saturday matinee. I was totally catalyzed as I considered the power of the mind. As was evidenced in the movie, a human being could do so much with a mind. The scientist had also manifested many positive things in his life. Whatever he concentrated upon for a short time would come into three-dimensional manifestation. He could manifest his daughter, for example, in miniature form within a crystal dome, and observe her as a projection of his mental image of her. It was a kind of futuristic, high-tech telepathic visualization. With even more astounding mental prowess, when the monster threatened, the scientist could surround his dwelling with those iron-fortified shields through the power of his focused awareness. Yet, even with all his demonstrated mastery, the mind ultimately eluded his control, as the darkness of his unconscious, personified as the monster, the manifestation of his own negative data, destroyed him.

The mind: such possibility, such potential! I was both excited and frightened at the challenge that lay before me. For even as a boy of eleven at the Saturday matinee, I, too, had a mind. What would become of me? The mind: positive or negative? Good or bad? Genius or mediocrity? The considerations seemed infinite, and I was as overwhelmed as any innocent eleven-year-old boy would be.

I contemplated the theme of the movie *The Forbidden Planet* for many years and progressively resolved its riddle. The mind is a subject that human beings have contemplated for thousands and thousands of years, and there is much documented information to explore throughout human history regarding it. My own exploration culminated for me in something Muktananda said one day. "Consider this," he said. "The mind: bondage or liberation?" He was commenting on ancient Eastern philosophy as it examined the mind in relation to the nature of reality. With this question as bait, he had my attention, and he proceeded to launch me into the daily study of the same philosophy. What exactly is the mind, and how does it function within the human condition? What is the brain, and how does it relate to the mind? What is an ego? What about surrender? Is liberation based on surrender, and without surrender is there endless bondage? What is surrendered, what is relinquished, what is transcended? Who does what to whom? What's it all about?

In order to understand surrender, we must first comprehend the specifics of the brain-mind and the ego. The mind is best understood in relation to its place within the nature of reality and its self-delighting expression that I have called the Creation Game. Source, as ultimate reality, is pure, eternally delighting creative awareness. It is consciousness itself. It is beyond polarity and inherently contains the basic informational principles essential to its nature as seed data within itself. Out of the pleasure of its eternally delighting creative awareness, for the fun of it, it polarizes itself into the seeming duality of the unmanifest and the manifest, the positive and the negative, or, more scientifically, matter and antimatter. The initial polarization maintains a perfect equilibrium, and through the still point of this balance, Sourceful awareness floods the creation. This is the threshold of the dual and the nondual, of unity and diversity, in which true reality as self-luminous, blissful creative awareness reveals itself to itself for the delight of itself. It is but a joyful play of consciousness. There is no dualistic separation of subject and object. It is the celebratory expression of Source as the Creation Game, a game, as all games, played for the fun of it.

As the playful, creative expression continues, balance densifies into imbalance, and from the tension of disequilibrium the subtle elements of matter and antimatter appear. Thus, unity is overwhelmed by diversity, and there is universal manifestation. The more the imbalance increases, the more diversified the manifestation becomes. Proportional to the increase in polarized tension is a decrease in unity awareness. Thus, as Source densifies itself into matter through the imbalanced stress of polar opposites, the awareness of itself is obscured. The manifestation appears dualistic, and a seeming separation of opposites is born of diminished nondual awareness. As imbalance increases to the extremes of polarized diversity, Sourceful awareness becomes even more obscured until it is fully concealed within itself. This, simply stated, is the Creation Game, a version of hide-and-seek Source plays with itself.

Yet, all games exist for the fun of it, and so does the Creation Game. Revelation is always possible. The true nature of Source contains the inherent principles that reveal itself to itself. Whenever balance returns, the luminosity of awareness as self-revelation expresses itself. The lost is found, the hidden is revealed, and within the revelation the pure bliss of being floods everything.

Thus, through many stages of increasingly diversified manifestation, Source creates itself as energy and as the gross elements that are the building blocks of the universe as we know it: from the quantum to the subatomic, from the atomic to the molecular and the cellular, until we appear in human forms. At the subtlest level, at the center of our manifest being, we are luminous particles of Source consciousness. We embody the polarity of unity and diversity. When balanced, we are self-luminous and aware. When imbalanced, we are extremely diversified and proportionately unaware.

Intrinsic to our nature as Source are the principles of balance and self-revelation, wherein we experience the radically pleasurable delight of pure awareness. It is instinctual to journey toward balance, for therein lies self-revelation and mastery of the Creation Game.

A variation of the story of the Creation Game that has been in circulation for some time, based on the Vedic tradition, personifies Source as a supreme being. In this case, we'll call the supreme being the Lord, who decides to create a game for his ongoing, eternal delight. He manifests the universe out of himself, which includes this earth. Then he creates the human being. The game he creates involves a riddle, the secret of which is hidden within it. The secret is that what humanity is looking for is within. The God humans are looking for, they also are.

When the Lord considers where to hide this secret so that it is difficult to find and insures the eternal continuation of the game, he contemplates many places. First he thinks, I'll put it at the bottom of the deepest ocean, but then he sees into the future of humanity and realizes that they'll create submarines and get down to the bottom of the deepest ocean and they might find it too easily. So, he realizes that this won't work. He then considers hiding the secret at the top of the highest mountain, but he looks into the future and sees that there will be mountain climbers going over Mount Everest and somebody might find it. Then he considers the moon, but he looks into the future and sees spaceships going to the moon. So, no, that won't work. Finally, he determines that humans will surely find the secret in all these places, and as he contemplates the matter further, he rejoices in coming up with the one place that humans will rarely look. He places the key in the center of the human being, in the human heart, for he knows that very few will ever look there. This, then, insures the eternal delight of the perpetuation of the Creation Game.

So what is the mind, and how does it appear within this Creation Game? According to the most ancient of philosophical systems, as well as the cutting edge of quantum mechanics expressed by modern physicists, the mind appears within the Creation Game when the intrinsic data of unity within Source meets itself as the data of the diversity that comes about through the process of manifestation. This is the mind as pure database. The spontaneous creativity of Source insures the interaction of data, and through ever-unfolding diversification, the mind as a database increases its entangled intricacies, data upon data, information within information, billions upon billions of intricate combinations and possibilities of continuously unfolding data.

The mind as database is thus a level of manifested reality and forms part of the creation that is the particle at the core of all form. Most specifically, it is the particle at the center of human experience. As the individual particle explores the diversity of manifestation through the human form, the creative expression of data unfolds. The possibilities of interaction are endless, and the game is truly creative and spontaneous. No two journeys could possibly be the same. Such is the vast diversity of manifestation. As truly unique data are formed in this seemingly individual process, they are stored in the memory banks of the mind as a database. Thus, each particle, through its memory banks, assumes a unique individuality based on its journey within the Creation Game.

As this unique individuality is formed through the creation of a personalized memory database, identification follows. Responses to stimuli are stored in memory, and when a similar stimulus appears, memory is scanned and the stored response repeated. A familiar example is the rush of emotions that can accompany a scent recognized from childhood. This is patterned, memorized repetition and automated behavior. It entails the absence of pure, spontaneous creative expression. As patterns of repetition are built within the individual database, we become identified with these patterns of memorized response, and attachment follows. Then, through identified attachment, subject seemingly separates from object, and the duality of observer and observed as disconnected and distinct appears.

To put this in terms of contemporary psychology, the baby who is born in a perfect state of equilibration and oneness, known as symbiosis, through the first two years of life becomes conditioned to a world of subject and object, in a process known as separation-individuation. Thereafter, as development continues, the child's lower frequency of brain waves make the child particularly susceptible to subconscious programming up to the age of puberty, by which time the ego and its dualistic illusions are firmly entrenched.

This is the manifestation of the ego within the Creation Game of hide-and-seek. But remember, it is only a game for the fun of it. The mind and the ego are necessary for the playing of the game. When they are relinquished, as hiding and seeking balance each other, subject and object merge, and we experience revelation as pure, nondual Source awareness once again appears in all its fullness. This is like the sun reappearing from behind the clouds as the sky clears.

So what is surrender? In this context, it is merely the relinquishment of our unconscious identification with the repetitive patterns of memorized data that obscure our pure awareness of Source. It is the relinquishment of the ego and the entangled diversifications of repetitive and limited brain-mind data. This is the constant challenge of the Creation Game, and herein lies the key to its mastery. Whenever there is equilibration, whenever subject balances object, antimatter balances matter, and the right brain balances the left brain, we simplify our diversity in relation to our unity, minimize polarization, and ultimately transcend duality as nondual Source awareness alone remains. The journey, then, is one of balance, to manifest that equilibrium of being that inevitably delivers the radical pleasure of Source revelation, wherein we experience the bliss of freedom.

In my early days with Muktananda in India, I immediately noticed this new balance and a proportional expansion in my awareness. The living conditions at the ashram were spartan and basic. We engaged in a simple monastic lifestyle, and as a Westerner addicted to creature comforts, I could have found the transition challenging. In winter we arose at two in the morning and began the day with a bath. The bathhouse was not heated, and the vents were permanently open. Water was heated in a wood-fired boiler and dispensed one bucket per person. We then mixed this with cold water and, squatting naked in the bath stall, poured the water over our bodies with a small dipper. With an early morning temperature of forty degrees, the only heat available came from the steam rising from our bodies in the cold stone bathhouse. This was a real morning awakener! Then, during the five-month monsoon season, it rained nearly every day. Nature surrounding the ashram quickly became tropical, and every species of insect multiplied in abundance. Since there were no screens on the windows, sleeping could have been a real challenge with all my conditioned data about comfort. But, somehow, none of this mattered as much as I thought it would. Elevated in the presence of Muktananda's Source-field, I became a detached observer of my own mind. Within this balance, my awareness expanded, and I began to witness the movie of my life, rather than identify with it. As a result, misery was replaced with bliss, and I enjoyed the pleasurable experience of true freedom. In this way, progressively over the years, I validated for myself the principle of balanced transcendence.

In a related anecdote from the Zen tradition, we find an enlightening monk who was traveling through the countryside. Suddenly, it started to rain. As the monk continued along, the rain intensified. In the distance, he saw a monastery with a small temple. As he approached, the monks welcomed him. Since the living quarters were full, they said to him, "You can stay here in the temple." Night fell, and it got colder. Our enlightening monk noticed that the idol of Buddha at the front of the temple was made of wood. He took it, broke it up, and built a fire to warm himself. Soon he was warm and comfortable. But the head monk and the other brothers noticed the smoke and came running. When they saw that the fuel for the fire was their wooden statue of Buddha, which was a valuable antique, they were outraged. Amazed and angry, they threw the enlightening monk out into the bitterly cold night. In the final scene, our enlightening monk was sitting under a tree, cold, but with a look of bliss and happiness on his face.

This story shows how we can become so identified with our data that we throw the real God, the truthful awareness of Source, away, as we cling to our silly concepts. We get upset, while the enlightening being remains constant in the balanced state of nondual awareness, and hence blissful.

Now let us reconsider our scientist in the MGM movie. Obviously, he hadn't mastered being human. He certainly did not demonstrate any balanced transcendence. Rather, he personified imbalance as he remained egotistically identified with his brain-mind database. Since his personal database was dominantly negative, he manifested the ultimate self-negation; he annihilated himself. The monster was only the play of his negative programming empowered by his ego. It could be said that he committed suicide. Yet, it's all only a movie, and our scientist will more than likely manifest additional chances at mastery in the continued playing of the game.

To understand this fully, for a moment we must step beyond the framework of one human life cycle. One full cycle of the Creation Game does not correspond to one human life cycle. The manifested cycle of true reality, including an infinite number of life cycles, is like the day of Source. It is followed by the unmanifest cycle, as the night of Source. Nothing is perpetuated between these games of cosmic dimensions. From dual perception in linear time and space, each game might last many hundreds of billions of years. So there could be many cycles of the game within the game. There could be many human cycles within the game throughout one manifested cycle of the full Creation Game. Perhaps the major impressions within one cycle of human experience are stored in memory and are cumulative with the particle or soul throughout its journey in a full manifested cycle of the Creation Game.

If you do not master the game in one cycle, there will be many more journeys in which you can perfect your playing of the game. Ultimately, you master the game through maintaining a constant state of balance and Source awareness. Thereafter, throughout the remaining manifested cycle, you continue the play as a master of the game for the fun of it. The game would just become more intricately focused, for ever greater delight. Since Source is nondual, there is no beginning or end, but rather an eternal forever in which there will always be more. After each manifest and unmanifest cycle, all data are dissolved, and only ultimate reality as pure awareness remains. Then a whole new Creation Game appears, totally unique and incomparable to any other Creation Game because of the inherent creative spontaneity.

In the final understanding, nothing is really perpetuated between games. Continuance and progression are only illusions within the manifested cycle of a game and appear so because of the duality of time and space. Beyond time and space, beyond the dual illusion, nothing is perpetuated. In the truth of the eternal now, revealed through equilibration, only awareness is real. All else is insignificant and meaningless, and we only fool ourselves that there is an ongoing perpetuation. It is simply arrogance on the part of an ego assuming a false authority over consciousness for continued existence. Whatever happens will be a surprise, and whether or not we are aware, the game remains intrinsically delightful.

When all is said and done, an innate expression of our freedom is our awareness that reality is meaningless. It's just a game, and the key is simplification, an aware observation at the still point between the manifest and the unmanifest, wherein duality yields to nonduality and reality as pure awareness in all its freedom alone is. As the sage Ashtavakra wrote in the ancient Indian text the Ashtavakra Gita, "One who fixes his mind to freedom is free, as is one who fixes his mind to bondage bound. There is the truth in the saying 'Like intention, like becoming.'" We are bound when we remain identified with our ego-mind. Once we surrender this identification, we begin to taste the sweet nectar of freedom that arises from a truthful awareness of the nature of Source as the Creation Game.

CHAPTER 9

Transcending Ego Identification

Freedom requires no rehearsal.
Conceptualization is rehearsal.
It negates experience.
It cannot solve the problem.
It is the problem.

MASTER CHARLES

As we play the Creation Game, when we show minimal awareness during the current cycle of our human journey, we'll probably end up having a miserable time. This was the case with our movie scientist described in the last chapter. When awareness contracts, so does delight. This is the ego's plight: misery, suffering, and the absence of any real or lasting pleasure within the Creation Game. From the perspective of nondual Source awareness, the ego is very entertaining with its attendant and limited brain-mind database. But, from the perspective of the ego, it's all just relentless misery, fuel for the quest of mastery within the Creation Game. The wise would surely realize that help is needed. But where is the "help key" in the midst of all this data? Where does one get assistance within the Creation Game?

Perhaps the movie scientist would have benefited from having an enlightening master, someone to show him the way. But that would have entailed an entire rewrite of the script, and the outcome would have been completely different. All of the mystical traditions concerned with human mastery emphasize the importance of a master in one's journey. If you want to master anything, it would seem desirable to find someone who has mastered it already and then learn from that master's experience. An enlightening master is one who has mastered the Creation Game and is living an equilibration of being, simplified and quiescent at the still point of human existence. The master's state of being demonstrates a mastery of the ego and brain-mind. The master's reverberation as a multidimensional energy offers an entrainment to all who would journey the same.

This is easy to understand in a scientific context. All form has frequency, which is the rate of oscillation within its polarity. Each human form has its own unique frequency of reverberation based on the exact degree of its polarization. This can easily be observed at the cellular level. The denser the form or the more identified it is with repetitive, dualistic data, the faster the frequency of reverberation. The more subtle the form or the less identified it is with dualistic data, the slower the frequency of reverberation. Since expansion of awareness in the Creation Game is proportional to the relinquishment of ego identification with limited, dualistic data, the slower frequency corresponds with a more expanded, nondual awareness. Thus, those who have transcended dualistic ego identification would have the slowest frequency of reverberation. Since the lowest frequency has the highest amplitude, or the greatest impact on its environment, such masters would offer a low-frequency entrainment to everyone and everything in their environment. Just like tuning forks, such masters would entrain all surrounding frequencies to their frequency.

The principle of frequency and amplitude can easily be validated in an observation of the human brain. The brain is divided into two sides, right and left, which also correspond to the two sides of the body. The right brain and the left brain represent a duality. When they are imbalanced in function, the brain-wave frequency is accelerated. When they are more balanced in function, there is a proportional deceleration in brain-wave frequency. This is termed *whole-brain synchronization*. In general, human beings use less than 10 percent of their brain capacity, and this is evidenced by their imbalanced hemispheres and very accelerated brain waves.

When focus is introduced to the brain, as in meditation, whole-brain synchrony increases, and the brain waves decelerate. Since the low frequency has a higher amplitude, there is more impact upon the brain, and its function increases upward from the tenth percentile. This is marked by paranormal or nonordinary states of experience. One aspect of this process is that the brain secretes more of its natural neurochemical opiates, and the person becomes intoxicated or blissful. This bliss is directly proportional to the expansion of awareness. If there is constancy of whole-brain synchronization and decelerated brain-wave frequency, the person remains proportionately expanded in blissful awareness. Also, the low-frequency vibration becomes an entrainment to anyone or anything in that person's environment. Thus, equilibration within the human brain diminishes dual polarity and expands nondual awareness. The basic principles of the Creation Game remain the same within the microcosm as they are within the macrocosm.

In scientific experiments conducted by the French researcher Alain Aspect in the early 1980s, it was proved that reality as we think we know it does not exist. The universe of solid matter is an illusion. It is the molecular structure of particles that appears to be solid. At the subatomic level, however, there is no separation; all is one. Further, the molecules with which we manifest our physical reality are organized by electromagnetic fields of energy. We are each a field of energy organizing the molecular structures that we perceive as physical reality. We all can learn to manipulate our reality by manipulating our electromagnetic field of energy.

Further scientific investigation has revealed that there is one thing that can distort the electromagnetic fields of energy. That one thing is thought. Thus, human beings can consciously or unconsciously manipulate their reality through the particular orchestration of their thought patterns. What is observed, then, is distorted by the data of the observer. A simple story that illustrates this distortion principle tells of a group of ten scientists standing in a line. The first scientist whispers into the ear of the scientist next to him, "Oxygen." That scientist whispers the word into the ear of the next, and so it passes down the line, similar to the children's game of "Telephone," until the word

emerges from the mouth of the last scientist, who ex-
claims, "Helium!"

Mysticism has long maintained that we manifest our reality based on our data. Science now concedes that electromagnetic thought patterns are a field of energy that
directly affects what is observed. As the physicist Amit
Goswami puts it in his book *The Self-Aware Universe*,
"Mental experiences, such as thought, do not seem to be
material, so we have developed a dualistic philosophy that
relegates mind and body to separate domains. The short-
comings of dualism are well known. Notably, it cannot explain how a separate, non-material mind interacts with a
material body. If there are such mind-body interactions,
then there have to be exchanges of energy between the
two domains."

Thought, then, can be considered a form within a form.
It also carries a frequency based on its specific degree of
dual polarization. The individual frequency of any form is
based on the dual to nondual ratio of its database. If people are egotistically identified with extremely dualistic
data, their energetic frequency would be very accelerated.
By the same token, enlightening masters, who are beyond
ego identification, would display a very decelerated energetic frequency. Their very frequency of reverberation
would be a radically decelerated, high-amplitude entrainment for all in their environment, a very powerful tuning
fork. What then would be the result?

Since all forms within proximity would be entrained to
the master's slow frequency of reverberation, all that was
incongruent with such frequency would have to be relinquished. In other words, all egotistically identified, dual-

istic data would have to shift and move to more nondual frequencies to be harmonic to the master's. Otherwise, the stress would be too great and the disharmony of proximity would be too intense. Thus, as dualistic data shift and are relinquished, stress dissipates and with increased balance there is a pleasurable harmony. It is a necessary and inevitable process intrinsic to the Creation Game.

Surrender, then, is really a natural process whenever there is an equilibrated entrainment within one's environment. If such an equilibrated entrainment remained a constant in one's environment, there would be a progressive relinquishment of the egotistically identified dualistic database until the frequencies were matched and merged. All that would remain would be pure awareness, or Source consciousness. All divergent frequencies would have merged into the balanced state of blissful freedom. This is the nature of true surrender. It is a natural process within the Creation Game.

It is for the sake of this process that enlightening masters appear within the Creation Game. Their very frequency of reverberation equilibrates all in their environment and entrains all form to Source revelation. This spells human mastery and is the culmination of the Creation Game. Whenever a particle or soul manifests a certain degree of equilibration through a form, as demonstrated by its frequency of reverberation, the master as a harmonic frequency must appear. This is really a process of self-revelation, and the master is but a reflection of the most fully aware dimensions of oneself. The final degrees of frequency alteration that such a reflection brings about are an intricate and delicate surgery and a radical human experience. This process is no less than the total relinquishment of the ego and its limited, dualistic database. It is no less than the self-deliverance of the ultimate bliss of freedom.

Muktananda was obviously such a reflection for me, and through the delicate surgery he performed, I journeyed through the final relinquishments of ego identity and attachment to dualistic data. Day after day, year after year, the entrainment continued, until I revealed myself to myself for the blissful delight of self-revelation.

Throughout the journey, I diligently watched the progressive shifts in my database from dual to nondual. This could easily be observed in my beliefs regarding deity. I began with God as Mother, dualistic and limited, and progressed to God as Mother, unlimited as the Creator of all and everything, the manifest polarity in consciousness that is one with the unmanifest polarity, and through equilibration merges in absolute oneness as the pure awareness of ultimate reality. This progressive journey was intricately facilitated through the energetic entrainment of Muktananda's enlightening reverberation as it appeared and remained a constant in my environment. Ultimately, I liberated myself, and in the merging we were one, but there were attachments to ego data and repetitive patterns of behavior along the way that required masterful assistance to cut through the bondage of limitation and deliver the expansive awareness of equilibrated being. Such is the role of the true master.

The enlightening master both exemplifies truthful awareness and awakens all to the absurdity of their dualistic thought process. In one story, a group of monks is gathered in the village square, having a philosophical debate about subjectivity and objectivity. They're arguing back and forth, back and forth. It so happens that an enlightening master is walking by and overhears their debate. He strolls up, listens for a while, then interrupts them. "Your debate is about subjectivity and objectivity. Tell me this: You see that big stone over there? Would you say that stone is inside your mind or outside?" Well, the monks consider the point, and they debate it back and forth, back and forth, and finally they elect a spokesperson, who says, "Since philosophically speaking, everything is an objectification of the mind, therefore, that stone is inside my mind." Whereupon the enlightened master says, "Well, you must have a very heavy head if you have a big stone like that inside it!"

The mind will never deliver truth to us; we can't get it by thinking. The ego's attachment to limited data must be relinquished, and this surrender requires assistance from the master. When I first accompanied Muktananda on a tour of the West, he held a weekend meditation retreat in northern California. I was not yet his personal secretary, so I was able to participate in the retreat. I had been strictly vegetarian for many years and was currently following Zen macrobiotics as a specific diet. I decided that this would be an appropriate time for a ten-day brown rice fast. In Zen macrobiotics, the brown rice fast is considered optimum for equilibration of the physical body polarities and results in the maintenance of perfect health and harmonic awareness. I planned the ten-day fast so that it would culminate on the final day of the retreat with Muktananda.

I had done the fast many times with great success, and this time was no different. Everything was perfect, and the meditation retreat over the final three days was very expansive. By the last day, I was feeling very accomplished in myself and was silently celebrating my brilliance for having journeyed it with such perfection. If ever an ego was inflated, here was the perfect example!

At the end of the last session with Muktananda, we had an opportunity to greet him and receive his formal blessing. A long line formed, and one by one everyone slowly approached his seat. When I finally got to the front of the line, I observed the person ahead of me having his exchange with Muktananda, the conclusion of which was the gift of a large piece of chocolate candy. Muktananda was giving everyone who came forward to greet him a piece of candy along with his blessing.

Now what could be more inappropriate to a ten-day brown rice fast than a piece of chocolate? I certainly had no intention of taking the chocolate and ruining my current state of fasting equilibration. So when Muktananda offered me the chocolate, I simply said, "No thank you!" He looked quite surprised, because in his tradition a gift of food from the master is considered very special, and even a fool would never refuse. Again he offered me the chocolate, as if he had misunderstood my refusal, and this time I said, "No thank you, I'm fasting." He responded that a meditator should never fast completely, but should always eat just one food. Again, he offered me the chocolate, and again I refused. Finally, with focused intensity, he said, "Eat this," and grabbing my hand, pushed the chocolate into it.

As I got up and slowly walked back to my seat, all my ego resistance surfaced in an instant. Muktananda had catalyzed me to the breaking point. Surely, I thought to myself, he does not know what he is doing. No one would interrupt a ten-day brown rice fast with a piece of chocolate, and furthermore, anyone who had any understanding of health, well-being, and human mastery whatsoever would never eat a piece of chocolate at all. It was pure poison from a macrobiotic viewpoint and could only ever deliver ill health from the imbalance that it would cause in the human body. On and on I silently raged within myself as I stared at this gooey lump of chocolate melting in my hand and ran every type of data about food, diet, health, mastery, and misery that had accumulated in my database over eons of time. The chocolate became the focal point of all my invested inadequacy, and I was immobilized with egotistical attachment.

When I finally sat down, I was so miserable from the stress of my own mind in the moment that all the bliss of the ten-day brown rice fast and the weekend retreat had completely vanished. But somehow, in the depths of my despair, the clouds seemed to part for an instant, and I got a glimpse of myself in the process and how I was creating the whole mess. My awareness expanded, and suspended in momentary witness consciousness, I heard a familiar voice reverberate within me with all its motherly love and simply say, "Surrender and just eat the chocolate!" Locked within this silent time warp, my mind relinquished all thinking, and as the ego resistance dissolved, I popped the chocolate into my mouth.

In an instant, liquid bliss flooded my entire being as if the chocolate were really some hallucinogenic drug in disguise. Higher and higher I soared until everything was just a scintillating, luminous play of consciousness before me. I was peaceful, blissful, and full of love. No brown rice fast had ever delivered this high an experience! I was amazed at what a little surrender could manifest. It seemed so simple. Once my limited thinking was set aside, awareness expanded to truthful freedom. Muktananda was absolutely brilliant in the journey of surrender that he facilitated with that little piece of chocolate!

This again is the demonstration of the true mystical master. He calls attention to the absurdity of your data and assists you in seeing how you limit yourself. Then follows surrender, and through enlightening entrainment Sourceful awareness expands and the ego is slowly dissolved. The result is progressive freedom.

There is another story from the Zen tradition that I often tell to illustrate a similar point: that it is a master's enlightening entrainment that annihilates the ego and forever alters the content of the brain-mind database.

Once upon a time, there was a very renowned philosopher. His intellectual brilliance was well acknowledged and he traveled far and wide to debate the learned philosophers of his day. His ego was vast and continued to fuel his conquests. It so happened that an enlightening master lived as the head of a nearby monastery, and arrangements were made for the philosopher to meet him in a debate. The day dawned, and the meeting took place in the great hall of the monastery. A table was set on a raised dais with two chairs. On the table sat a teapot and two cups.

The philosopher and all his followers entered first and took their seats. The enlightening master soon appeared and also took his seat. After a long silence, the master picked up the teapot and began pouring tea into the philosopher's cup. The cup was soon filled and began to overflow, and still the master continued to pour the tea. It filled the saucer and then overflowed and began to drip off of the table onto the floor. Still the master continued pouring.

Finally, when he could stand it no more, the philosopher interrupted the master, saying, "Stop! Can't you see it's full!" Whereupon the master replied, "Like this cup, you are too full of thoughts, concepts, and beliefs. How can I show you the truth unless you first empty your cup!"

The point is obvious. The philosopher was lost in his ego identification with all his philosophical brain-mind data. He was imbalanced and nonaware. He had only a vast amount of limited and diversified data, which he could repeat from memory. His was a purely dualistic experience. He was no match for the enlightening master, who lived in balance and was constant in Source awareness. The master's expression simply demonstrated enlightening awareness and won the match before any debate even began. If the philosopher was at all attentive, he would have recognized the enlightening master's truth and asked him for guidance. With continued assistance, he would have transcended the ego and enjoyed the bliss of freedom.

CHAPTER 10

The Mind: Bondage or Liberation?

*Clouds are brought in by the wind and driven out by the wind,
so also is humanity's bondage caused by the mind,
and so also is its liberation.*

SHANKARACHARYA

I immediately recognized Muktananda's truthful expression. His balanced state of being was demonstrated daily in his very powerful decelerated energy entrainment. My ego could not mistake this presence for anything other than what it was. It was a mastery that demanded challenge, but could never be conquered, yet my unconscious ego continued its manipulative repetitions over the many years of our journey together. In so many ways, for twelve years, Muktananda was like the enlightening master with his teapot, demanding that I awaken, empty myself, become still and attentive, and ultimately transcend the ego's brain-mind identity. He demanded attention to the truth of oneness at all times through his constantly aware expression. Whenever my ego identification appeared, he called my attention to it, and in the process I relinquished it through a radical expansion of awareness. This is always a mark of the enlightening master. Transformation comes through awareness. It is the master's natural state of being. Once, Muktananda and company were traveling and presenting programs in the southwestern United States. In this instance, we were in Albuquerque, New Mexico. While traveling, we maintained a small staff, and each of us performed many roles. I was personal secretary and man Friday. The place where the seminar was presented was a fifteen-minute drive from where we were staying, and my job was to drive Muktananda to and from the program, and be his attentive assistant throughout the day. As we were leaving for the program, his personal attendant handed me a towel with his drinking goblet and a can of Coca-Cola wrapped within it. Muktananda would be drinking Coca-Cola during his break in the program, and I was supposed to serve it to him in the privacy of his waiting room at the appropriate time. I took the towel and placed it on the backseat of the car and drove Muktananda to the program.

After he went in, I parked the car and continued with my noble assisting. I was very ecstatic to have the highly coveted job as personal secretary and certainly wanted to be the best I could possibly be, demonstrating my attentiveness in all situations. However, just before the break came in the program, I realized that I had left the towel with the goblet and Coca-Cola in the car. With barely enough time, I slipped out of the room during the meditation, ran out to the car, got the towel, and ran all the way back to the reception room, hoping to beat Muktananda to it and appear ready, attentive, and accomplished.

It was a very hot day, and the car sitting in the direct sun was blazing hot inside. I was sweating when I returned to the waiting room just before Muktananda arrived for his break. I wiped the telltale sweat from my face and neck and pretended to be cool, calm, and collected as he entered the room. Muktananda sat in his chair and asked for the Coca-Cola. I unwrapped it from the hot towel and handed him the goblet to hold so I could open the Coca-Cola and pour it for him. I never even considered that the Coca-Cola was hot in the can from being in the car and that I had run with it under my arm all the way from the parking lot to the waiting room. I was too concerned with appearing to be the most impressive assistant on the planet! Well, when I pulled the tab on the can, hot, bubbly Coca-Cola exploded all over Muktananda. It was dripping from his glasses, from his nose, from everywhere, and it had splattered all over his clothes, even down to his shoes.

I was totally upset! I lost all my focused facade, and my mind ran away at warp speed with every scenario possible. All my negative data surfaced as I considered what to do next. Muktananda just sat there motionless with the Coca-Cola dripping from him. I decided that perhaps I should try to blot the messy liquid and dry him off, but I was too immobilized with fear to do anything. I had just demonstrated that I was a total idiot by spraying Coca-Cola all over the master. Surely, he would replace me as his assistant, and I would be denounced forevermore. On and on my mind raced. Muktananda waited until I attained my absolute peak and, with impeccable timing, without batting an eyelash, he simply looked at me and said, "Obviously, you don't know much about Coca-Cola!"

My mind stopped immediately. It came to a screeching halt within the present moment as all fear was suspended in the awareness of his enlightening presence, which seemed to expand radically and completely engulf me.

Time and space seemed to dissolve, as, poised in stillness, I became a witness to the situation as it was unfolding. I was expanded beyond the mere physical dimension and understood with absolute clarity exactly what he had just said. The whole of my being was saturated with intoxicating bliss. I was fully balanced, and the absurdity of my brain-mind data and the ego's identification with it became absolutely hilarious. From this dimensional shift in perception, everything was simply entertaining. Enjoying the laughter reverberating in every cell of my being, I simply picked up the towel and blotted Muktananda dry, poured the remaining Coca-Cola into the goblet for him to drink, and prepared him to return to the program when the break was over. I remained high on expanded awareness for the rest of the day, and incredible shifts occurred in my database from this simple teaching.

Long after I had returned Muktananda to his quarters for the night, I remained in a euphoric state of blissfully peaceful observation. I was mesmerized with the natural spontaneity of shifting data that was catalyzed by a silly can of Coca-Cola. Again, I was in awe of Muktananda. What had he really meant when he said, "Obviously, you don't know much about Coca-Cola!"? Coca-Cola was the symbol for the Creation Game. From my programmed reaction, it was easy to see that I was not very aware. I had lost all focus because of my ego identification with limited data, and I had relinquished true awareness. I revealed that I was without mastery and had very little truthful understanding of the nature of reality as well. If I had been fully aware, I would have remained still within, a calm witness to the diversity of the situation. I would not have lost my unity to the imbalanced polarity of diversity. I would have been blissfully entertained as a witnessing play of consciousness. With his statement, Muktananda drew me attentively to his balanced state of being, wherein I experienced pleasurable delight filling me to overflowing as I shared in his truthful awareness.

Muktananda was always laughing. His was not dualistic laughter, but a subtler laughter that reverberated in his very cells. It was the delight of constant awareness of Source. It could easily be seen in his eyes, which were always bubbling with blissfully intoxicated delight, as if he was seated in the audience and the play he was watching was the funniest comedy ever performed. It seemed that for him everything was entertaining, and a gentle yet revealing smile was always upon his lips.

It was interesting to me that Muktananda wore sunglasses most of the time. His eyes were certainly sensitive from all his years of meditation, but it seemed there was more to it than that. I used to watch people when they came up close to greet him or consult with him about their situations. Many were experiencing difficult challenges and were very seriously involved in their own dramas. Looking into his sunglasses, they could not see his eyes very clearly, and so they missed the laughter that was eternally present therein. If they could have seen the laughter and blissful delight, this might have upset their seriousness all the more. What could be worse than wanting compassion and sympathy for your problems and getting laughter and nonserious delight instead? The glasses were thus a kind of camouflage that allowed people to reflect their projections back upon themselves until such time as they were ready to relinquish them and experience for themselves the bliss of freedom. Whenever people would expand in awareness in his presence, he would remove his glasses and let them see his laughing eyes. This allowed a mutual delight and the most truthful commentary on the moment that he could give. It was an amazing process to watch.

Again and again he would say, "The world is as you see it," quoting an ancient philosophical treatise by one of his favorite enlightening sages, Vashishta from the Yoga Vashishta. He taught me that we project our own version of reality through our ego identification with specific data. What we think is what we get. We rarely observe what truthfully is, rather opting to obscure it with our version of what we think is real. We flavor everything with our particular beliefs and concepts. If these beliefs are dualistic and limited, then the world we create for ourselves is limited and dualistic. If these are nondual and truthful, then the world we create for ourselves is truthful and free. "The mind: bondage or liberation?" Muktananda would repeat, reminding us that the answer was determined by our ego identification with the mind or our transcendence of it to pure witness consciousness.

I like to consider it in this way: As one Source consciousness, we are the eternally aware witness. We witness as awareness the polarization of unity and diversity. Through imbalance, we diversify to the stressful extreme, yet as a balanced witness, we are only entertained by the play. Whether the data are positive or negative, comic or tragic, makes no difference to the witness.

When you go to the theater and sit in the audience, you can be equally entertained by the play whether it is a comedy or a tragedy. After the show, you realize that you were entertained as an audience witness. The problem is that most people cannot remain in the audience of their own plays. They keep jumping up on the stage and interacting with the actors, becoming identified with the comedy or the tragedy that is their projected life. If we did this in the theater, people would say we were crazy. Yet, the majority of us do this every day, and everybody thinks it is normal.

If we could just be a witness to our own minds and the play of our own data and relinquish identification with them, we would remain blissfully entertained in every moment. Descartes's famous statement, "I think, therefore I am," should truthfully be reversed to read, "I am, therefore I think," for the fun of it. From the truthful perspective of Source consciousness as a fully aware witness, all and everything is simply entertainment for our ongoing blissful delight.

There is a short tale of a monk who clearly understood the entertainment value of the mind's silliness. This smart monk opened a booth at the charitable fair for his monastery. "Any two questions, one hundred dollars" read the sign above the booth. Someone came up and handed over the money and asked, "One hundred dollars is very expensive, isn't it?" "Yes," replied the monk. "What's your next question?"

I am also reminded of another story from the Zen tradition. It seems that there was a group of monks gathered at the village center having a philosophical debate. They were standing at the base of a flagpole and discussing what made the flag flap. It just so happened that an enlightening master was passing by and overheard their debate. He stopped and listened silently. The first monk said, "It is the relationship of the flag and the wind that makes the flag flap." The second one countered, "No, it is the combined relationship of the flag, the wind, and the pole that makes the flag flap," and the third added, "Perhaps it is merely the flag and the pole, and the wind is incidental." Their debate continued back and forth for several minutes, and when it had reached its peak, the enlightening master interrupted them, saying, "My dear brothers, it is neither the wind, the pole, nor the flag but rather your minds that flap!"

This is the nature of the Creation Game. The ego identification with the diversified data of the brain-mind becomes so entangled that it disturbs the balance. As our minds flap, awareness is obscured, and we are lost in our limited data projections. Life then is full of confusion, stress, and misery.

Once while traveling with Muktananda in Texas, we decided to take him to a wildlife preserve. It was a large sanctuary through which you could drive and observe the animals in their uncaged natural habitats. Muktananda loved animals of all kinds, and we wanted him to have some time off from all the public and programs, so it seemed a good idea. The problem was that it rained very heavily every day, and we could not go. He was like a little child about it. Each morning he would ask me if we would go that day, and I would say that it depended on the rain. Finally, on the last day possible for our excursion, the clouds seemed to part for a little while, and he called me. He indicated that it looked all right and we should go immediately. We telephoned and informed them we were coming, for he was to be treated as a VIP, and they had arranged many special presentations with the animals just for him.

Off we went. It was about a half-hour drive. His driver was driving, I was in the other front seat, and Muktananda was riding by himself in the backseat. He remained silent, counting his divine name repetitions on his hand beads while riding in the car. I was diligently watching the sky and praying that the rain would not start again and ruin the whole trip. The sky was dark gray to my left, but the clouds were broken overhead. As we drove along, the gray horizon started to advance toward us like a massive wall of rain and storm. There were thunder and lightning in the distance. I prayed the harder and began to run my limited negative data on the absolute inappropriateness of the rain and how it would ruin the day and I would be held responsible for another mess.

The storm advanced, and the closer it came to the road, the more my mind ran completely out of control. As Muktananda sat in the backseat blissfully repeating his divine names, I sat in the front seat silently cursing the storm with every passing second. Then, just like a solid wall of gray pounding rain, it advanced to within twenty-five feet of the road and abruptly stopped, a drenching barrier of intensity, absolutely stalled. A few minutes of threatening challenge followed until it reversed direction and slowly retreated all the way back to the horizon. There it remained in the menacing distance while the sun came out overhead. Muktananda just continued to be still and repeat his divine names silently in the backseat. He never said a word.

In watching all this, I became very attentive. My mind stopped in awe of the miracle I had just witnessed. If it had just been left to my mind and ego, we certainly would have been rained out. But, Muktananda's balanced stillness was truly miraculous. Even the weather cooperated with this subtle harmony. I surrendered my controlling data and drifted into a meditative state, entrained again by Muktananda's energy dynamic, and expanded with blissful awareness. I became a quiescent witness to the ego's brain-mind and enjoyed the rest of the day in a state beyond compare. We toured the game preserve, and Muktananda delighted like a little child, especially when the lions jumped over his car to feed under the nearby trees. The sun remained and the rain abated until we returned to our retreat. Just before going into his quarters, Muktananda turned to me and said, "What nice weather; it didn't rain at all!" No sooner was the door closed behind him than the heavens opened, and it poured rain nonstop for the next twenty-four hours. As I joyfully reflected on all this, his words reverberated throughout my being: "It is as you see it! The mind: bondage or liberation!"

Being with Muktananda day after day in such close physical proximity was a profoundly expansive experience. His enlightening energy field was a powerful entrainment that always catalyzed a meditative synchrony within my being. Whether we were driving in a car, taking long walks, answering correspondence, giving meditation programs, or whether I was simply sleeping in a room adjacent to his, I felt the powerful effects of his presence. Little by little, day after day, the ego's brain-mind identification dissipated within this meditative Source-field, and I found myself more consistently aware and intoxicated with bliss.

It was like living a heaven on earth. Everything was becoming so beautiful, so magnificent. Life was joyful, and I was high and ecstatic beyond anything I could ever have imagined. This to me is the symbolism of the story of Adam and Eve. Through the imbalance of ego identification, awareness of Source is diminished and paradise is seemingly lost. Yet, whenever we are equilibrated and fully aware, heaven is revealed here and now as the consciousness of all and everything in the fullness of its divine delight. In so many ways, Muktananda entrained and entranced me with his enlightening reverberation, and life became the heavenly dream come true.

In the early days of our association at Muktananda's ashram in India, there were very few Westerners, and we lived a most disciplined lifestyle. We arose each day at 2:00 A.M., had a bath, exercised, chanted scripture, and then sat to meditate. The meditation room was adjacent to his quarters, and during the morning sessions he would join us on random occasions. He would walk around with a flashlight in hand and shine it on our heads as he touched us on the third eye vortex. In this focused way, he seemed to transmit his powerful decelerated energetic directly into us, and we would enjoy the most expansive of equilibrated meditations. Many times in these early sessions of meditation, my mind would be busy, and I could not maintain a meditative focus. Yet, as soon as he touched me, I would become still and transcendental. This is the mechanics of true meditation. It is a simplification process as the extremes of diversified data, characterized by the active mind, merge into balanced, still-point synchrony and transcend limited duality for the true freedom of pure awareness.

I would emerge from these incredible meditations absolutely high as if I were on drugs, blissfully elevated with a divine and weighty intoxication filling the whole of my being. It was such an all-inclusive and all-encompassing experience that I would not want to move for hours thereafter. I would somehow proceed to the next scheduled event, which was a two-hour chant with him over the dawn and into the morning, and the meditative expansion of awareness would continue to absolute oblivion. When it was over, I would stagger to my room. Lying upon the bed, I would disappear into the most subtle of transcendental states of unity awareness. Sometimes I would not be able to move from the bed for several hours as I was too rapturously inebriated to function in any physical way.

When I did emerge, I was so ecstatic and filled with enlightening awareness that I would just sit and witness this ineffable play of divine consciousness until I could make it to the next activity. Throughout the day we would work in the gardens, and following dinner Muktananda would feed us directly from his hands. We would line up and approach him one by one as he placed into our cupped hands varying special sweet preparations. Not only was the food good, a kind of special dessert, but it was another way in which he seemed to transmit his enlightening energy directly to us. All of these modalities of energetic transmission were well documented in his tradition, yet for us as Westerners, devoid of a living mystical tradition and experiencing this for the first time, it was amazing.

We would then proceed to the evening chanting session for an hour and a half, and thereafter retire to bed. It almost seemed as if the food that Muktananda gave us was laced with LSD or some hallucinogenic drug, because the experience we had thereafter was so expansive. But, truthfully, it was only filled with his enlightening frequency of reverberation, which decelerated and synchronized us into profound meditative states of transcendental awareness. In so many demonstrated ways, Muktananda seemed to live only for our transformation, and it was absolutely awe inspiring to be with him. Everything was so divine and conscious in his presence that Source became a palpable and real day-to-day experience. God and heaven were not some future fantasy to be fulfilled only if I was good, but rather a tangibly present reality that was my very existence. If Muktananda had manifested it for himself through the meditative journey, then it was possible that I could, too. With his living example expressed in every moment, I remained inspired to be all that it was possible for me to be. All I wanted was the constancy of divine communion, and I was increasingly consumed within this focus.

Over many years, my ego identifications and attachments seemed to dissolve within the synchrony of Muktananda's enlightening entrainment, and my database shifted to become congruent with the subtler dimensions of nondual Source awareness that I was experiencing. My daily meditations became increasingly more transcendental. I could sit for hours at a time, an aware witness in absolute abandon to ecstasy. Meditation was a twenty-four-hour-a-day experience in his energy field, and blissful awareness became a spontaneous, second-nature expression. I was constantly high on life lived within a truthful perception of what is. I was finding fulfillment. I was becoming the bliss of freedom.

I am reminded of another story that seems appropriate. Once there was a very enlightening monk who lived by the side of a river. He was very blissful and peaceful. Soon people from the nearby village came to know of him and gathered to experience his enlightening presence. Being thankful that he was with them, they would take care of him as best they could. Some brought food, some gathered flowers, and some built him a little hut to protect him from the weather. It was a beautiful expression of love. One day, however, the flower seller's daughter revealed that she was pregnant. When her parents pressed her to identify the father, she finally admitted that it was the enlightening monk. The word spread quickly, and soon a whole group marched out to see him at his hut. They displayed the pregnant daughter, accused the monk of being the father, insulted and abused him, and then asked him what he had to say. He sat quietly and only said, "Is that so!"

The months passed, and no one came to see him at all. When the baby was born, the flower seller and his wife brought it to him in their rage, and pushing their daughter's baby into his arms, told him that it was his responsibility to take care of it. They abused him some more, yet all he said was, "Is that so!"

The enlightening monk took care of the baby, nurturing it with love. All along, he remained constant in his blissful state of enlightening awareness. After a year and a half, the flower seller's daughter finally confessed that the real father wasn't the enlightening monk, but the butcher's son, whom she loved more than life itself and wanted to marry. The word spread, and everyone marched out to the enlightening monk's hut and demanded the return of the baby to its rightful parents. The enlightening monk, elevated within his state of true awareness, blissfully surrendered the child and simply said, "Is that so!"

The point is simple. If you are constant in Source awareness, beyond egotistical identification and limited dualistic data, you do not lose your balanced state of being in any situation. You remain a truthful witness, forever enjoying the play of consciousness as radical entertainment. You flow with each moment, like wind through a wheat field, the stress of resistance having long been surrendered to the ecstasy of peace. This is the state of human mastery, the enlightening state of mystical being, the state forever beyond the limitations of the ego's brain-mind. It is facilitated by true mystical masters. It is the bliss of freedom.

I remember a time a couple of years before his death when Muktananda continued his facilitation of my journey. He always said that I was an excellent public speaker, and over the years had continually praised my presentations in his programs. He always wanted me to introduce him because I did it well and made it easier for him in his presentations. He even made me teach public speaking to his other disciples to assist them with their program presentations. Everyone knew of his regard for me in this context. By this time there were many monks in training, and we rotated the speaking assignments in programs. Perhaps I would speak once in a month within the rotation of evening programs. One day, it was determined that one of the monks who was to speak in two days time was too ill to do it, and Muktananda suggested that I substitute for him.

I prepared as best I could for two days and delivered a very fine dialogue, which was clearly validated by the audience appreciation. Muktananda came into the program at the end of my presentation and proceeded to tell the whole audience that I was a fool. According to him, I had done everything wrong. I had not followed any of the appropriate speaker's protocols as designed by him. I had mispronounced the scriptural passages that I was quoting. I had gone overtime by a minute and a half, and so forth. On and on he continued, ranting and raving and seemingly denouncing me once and for all time. I sat in absolute stillness in my appropriate place within the audience as he addressed me and all through his program presentation and the meditation that followed. Thereafter, I silently returned to my room. No one ever asked me what I experienced. I am sure they were too concerned with their own data projections upon me to even inquire.

As for me, I had once again experienced Muktananda's focused transmission, which was very expansive. I had become constant enough in balanced awareness to remain a witness in whatever the situation, and this time was no different. I flowed with the moment and enjoyed the blissful delight of his energy field, which surrounded me and permeated me completely. I remained a witness and was entertained by the drama that he unfolded. It was nothing serious at all, just a silly play of consciousness for the fun of it. His eyes were still dilated with laughter, and I could see them through his dark glasses as they twinkled and conveyed a love for me more profound than anyone could ever imagine. Only egos are conditional. He was beyond ego, and the love he expressed was the true, unconditional love of one Source for itself as it celebrates itself as all and everything. We merged in the moments of our focused dance and delighted in the true stillness beyond all dualities. We were one within the bliss of freedom.

I knew he was pleased with me, and this was but another of his tests to see the state of awareness I had mastered. Yet, this time he did not have to explain it all to me afterwards. For in the play of the moment, he was clearly aware that we were one and free. We had journeyed closely together for many years, he and I, and these were the culminating days of all the entraining moments. We were one in the ecstasy of Source awareness.

As I sat within the quiet of my room all those years ago, filled with the wonder of Source consciousness, tears streamed from my eyes. Only a disciple can know such moments of love for the master. That he had so constantly and consistently given himself to me without condition was truly beyond any ego and mind's database to ever comprehend. He was truly an authentic enlightening master, and I loved him for the liberating reflection of myself that he embodied. Surrender was something that happened quite naturally during the special play of our association together.

"Always remember this," he said one day. "Wherever human beings gather together, there is separation, comparison, judgment, and delusion. It is only an illusion within the play of consciousness, and if you remain a truthfully aware witness you are forever free."

Here in these present moments, I am truthfully aware and I celebrate freedom as I witness these words blissfully dancing across the page in all their creative wonderment. Everywhere the play of consciousness delights before me. Scintillating and reverberating, glistening and dancing, it fills all and everything with its radiance and saturates the totality of what is with the ecstasy of its peace. It alone is, the one without a second . . . the bliss of freedom.

PART FOUR

LOVE

Love
The nature of Source
A reverberation of oneness
All and everything
In love with itself
Being and becoming
Neither you nor I
Just a truthful oneness
Here . . . now
Not a need, but an ecstasy
Blissfully enchanted
Peacefully fulfilled
A totality unto myself
I am love
I am
I

CHAPTER 11

Love Is All There Is

When you meet a true master,
he will awaken your heart
and show you the secret
of love and happiness.
KABIR

I had been with Muktananda about three and a half years and his personal secretary for over six months and was absolutely amazed at my journey with him. I had become so close to him on a daily basis, it was almost unbelievable. First of all I was a Westerner, and he was a traditional Eastern enlightening master, and the majority of those who surrounded him were also Easterners. Second, we had no common language and had to communicate through translators. As time passed, we developed forms of basic communication that left us free of translators, but for more complex communications, we always used them. Yet, in spite of these obstacles, we had become very closely associated. I was like one of his children, with access to his quarters, and I was intricately involved in his daily life. It was more than I could ever have dreamed possible, and I was ecstatic with the situation I had somehow manifested.

Muktananda was so magnificent and his energy field was so consistently radiant that I was very expanded in awareness and blissfully intoxicated because of my proximity to him. He was so pure, chaste, and saintly, a true example of the ultimate enlightening human being. I had placed him upon a very high pedestal, and for me he was becoming a deity. I had never met anyone who was so open and truthful and whose love was so absolutely unconditional. I loved and trusted him more than I had anyone in my whole life.

One day some urgent business appeared that demanded immediate attention. It was early evening, and Muktananda had retired to his quarters. He had his dinner around seven-thirty and thereafter remained in his room until he retired, usually no later than ten o'clock. We rarely disturbed him in the evening, but this was a special situation, and I needed to have his immediate decision. I went to his quarters and knocked at the downstairs door, but there was no answer. His personal assistant was not there, which seemed unusual, but since I had close association with him, I tried the door. It was open, so I decided to let myself in and see if he was available to handle the urgent business.

I entered and quietly climbed the stairs to the second floor, where I knew I would find him in his room. In these days, there was a drape across the doorway to his room. It was a cultural custom and also allowed his attendant to monitor him without totally invading his privacy. As I came up to the draped doorway, I thought I heard someone in the room with him. I stopped, listened, and affirmed that it was so, but the sounds I heard were not conversation. Rather, they were the sounds of two people being intimate.

I couldn't believe what I thought I was hearing, because of my lofty image of him, and moving closer to the door, I peered through the slit in the drapes before entering the room. What I saw stopped me cold in my tracks, and the bottom fell right out of my stomach—right out of my whole life. For there was Muktananda engaged in mutual sexual intimacy with one of his female assistants. I became absolutely still and silent. I was in shock. Slowly, I backed away from the door and ever so quietly made my way back down the stairs and out the entrance. I went to my nearby room and watched through emotional upheaval as my whole world crumbled around me and totally collapsed.

I couldn't sleep at all that night. My mind was racing at warp speed. I was sure that I had not been noticed, but I did not really care. How could this happen? How could I have been so stupid to have been fooled all along? Saints are supposed to be chaste and holy with vows of celibacy. Muktananda was a monk and he, too, had such vows. He taught celibacy and often talked of his own experiences regarding it throughout his spiritual journey. He had written extensively about it in his autobiography and encouraged all of us to practice true celibacy as the ultimate path. Somehow, I never questioned his adherence to his own teaching. I was sure that he was what he taught, that he "walked his talk," and that he was as pure as the driven snow on a winter day. But, what I had just seen with my own eyes had changed everything. My saint, my deity, had become a liar and a fraud—and I a fool.

Muktananda had taught us that there was a more truthful and pure love than that experienced in mere sexual relationships. It was love imbued with Source, immaculate and unconditional, the truthful reality of enlightening beings, the natural expression of unitive consciousness to be enjoyed through the meditative mastery of life. It was the stuff of mystics, saints, and sages. But, now I had discovered a flaw, one little thread that when pulled seemed to unravel the whole tapestry. Everything in me wanted to pack my bags and leave. I was in such a state of confusion that I just wanted to run away and forget the whole mess.

I suffered the night away alone in my room with my wild mind until it was six in the morning and time to meet Muktananda for the morning walk. I was too upset to do anything and too responsible to just disappear without explaining my departure, so I decided to adhere to the schedule until I could figure out some clear direction and decide what exactly to do. I met him for the morning walk, not knowing what to expect. He came out of his quarters as usual, and without saying anything we silently walked for an hour. Obviously, I had not been noticed the night before because he was acting perfectly normal, as if nothing unusual had happened.

My mind was still racing with all manner of possible scenarios as we began the walk, but after about ten minutes I noticed that I was intoxicated within the constancy of Muktananda's energy field. His enlightening reverberation, his mystical presence, was as palpable as ever before. It had not changed at all. If anything, it seemed even stronger this morning. The longer we walked, the higher I soared, and my mind with all its raging madness seemed to disappear into a far-removed distance, appearing as an intensely vibrating speck in the midst of a vast spatial expanse of nothingness. I was fully aware, absolutely inebriated with love, and as blissful as I had ever been.

By the time we returned, I was so drunk on love that my legs were like rubber, and I had to lie down in my room for a few minutes before being able to accompany Muktananda to the morning chanting program. Everything was swirling and hallucinating, pulsing and dancing, disappearing and reappearing—a delighting energy field in love with itself.

I continued through the day with my duties, elevated in this state of blissful love beyond compare and contemplated how it could be so. Why was Muktananda's state so constant if he were a fraud and a liar? If he was not practicing what he preached, if he was not a true master, why was his state of being, his energy dynamic, so powerful and unmistakably truthful? The constancy of such an enlightening state of being could not be faked. It had to be real if even when I had wanted to negate it, it had dominated my mind and entrained me into its synchrony. It could not be denied. It demanded to be challenged, but was unyielding in its thoroughly truthful demonstration. Obviously, then, he was not a fraud. But, at the same time, how was he truthful? My mind continued in this seemingly endless wrestling match, yet I could not deny the purity of energy that surrounded him. Muktananda's truth was greater than all my mental manipulations. His enlightening, Sourceful presence was unyielding.

Muktananda's truth, as demonstrated by the constancy of his energy field, was demanding a radical adjustment of everything in its environment, and that included me. A complete paradigm shift was in order. My database about love had to change because it was paralyzing me with conflict. This is always the case if we stagnate at an ego-level belief system. We must move toward a fuller awareness, where we can arrive at a new understanding that is congruent with our current reality. If we do not, we suffer the stress of resistance through ego attachment to our repetitive data.

There is a well-known story that illustrates the point. Once there was a monastery with many young monks in training. In their tradition, younger monks were assigned to older monks so that they would learn through association with a more mature illumination. It so happened that one such pair of monks was sent on a journey to a neighboring monastery. It was a three-day trip that took them through the mountains, into a valley and a large village, and then on to the monastery located in the mountains beyond. It was raining heavily as they set out walking along the mountain road. They walked in contemplative silence and spent the first night in a cave to shelter themselves from the rain.

The next day, they continued down the mountains and into the valley, eventually coming to the village. The rains had just lifted, but parts of the village were still flooded from the storm. They came to an intersection that was particularly muddy and wet, and therefore difficult to cross. There they encountered a beautiful young woman standing on the corner. Seeing the monks, she asked if they could help her cross the flooded road. The senior monk indicated his willingness and simply picked her up in his arms and carried her across the flooded intersection and deposited her on the other side. Bidding her farewell, he and the younger monk continued on their way.

They walked the rest of the day in continuing silence and at nightfall made their camp in the mountains. They prepared their meal and were about to settle down to sleep, when the younger monk could no longer contain himself and erupted with great intensity, saying, "How could you do it? We are not even supposed to look at a woman, much less touch one, and you went so far as to pick up that beautiful young woman and carry her across the intersection! This is completely unconscious. How could you do it?" Whereupon the older, more mature enlightening monk replied, "I left her back in that village. Why are you still carrying her?"

This story demonstrates the way it is when we are locked within our ego's database of entangled definitions. We cannot flow with what is happening, the play of the moment, but rather remain attached to our limited software and project it upon whatever is manifesting. We cannot allow the creative spontaneity of Source to be the way it is in all its diversity. With all our egotistical arrogance, we impose our restrictive data upon true reality and in so doing demonstrate our stressful, distorted, unconscious resistance. Instead, in such situations, we should endeavor to become still and balanced, and through expansion of our awareness arrive at creative spontaneity wherein appropriate shifts will happen naturally within our database.

In my case, Muktananda's constant enlightening energy field validated that he was anchored in truth and that the flaw was with me. There was definitely a glitch in my software regarding love, sex, and Source, and in order to relinquish the stressful imbalance in all its intensity, I needed to make a paradigm shift. Meditation was necessary to restore the balance so that a truthful awareness would reveal the movement that was necessary to relinquish the stress. This is exactly what happened as I walked that morning with Muktananda. His truthful reverberation entrained a meditative balance in me, and I expanded in awareness to a new perspective on the reality of the moment. I observed newly, creatively, with regard to the reality of love, sex and Source. Radical shifts were catalyzed over the next several days, and their reverberations continued for many years as my limited, dualistic data yielded to more truthful, nondual understanding. My awareness expanded, and the natural expression of true love replaced the fraudulent conceptual limitations with which I had paralyzed it. The bliss of freedom, all-encompassing and unlimited, expressed itself as love within the totality of Source.

Within the consistency of Muktananda's enlightening environment, I progressively experienced a paradigm shift in my limited database regarding love. Duality yielded to nonduality, and the paralysis of mental and emotional conflict lifted and disappeared. With love it seems somewhat easy, but what about sex? With all our Western puritanical conditioning, this is certainly the most challenging data to shift. The transformation offers a radical journey for anyone who allows it to unfold; so it was for Muktananda, and so it was for me. It is a progressive shift from dual to nondual and ultimately culminates in freedom.

Being in daily proximity to an enlightening master is a challenge not only to one's ego and limited database, but also to one's physical body. The frequency of the energy vibration is very decelerated, and this has a large impact on the body. In contemporary scientific understanding, this is termed an *enriched environment,* and is studied for its effect on the human brain. The low frequency with its high amplitude synchronizes the brain and slows the brain waves. In response, the pineal gland, the master gland of the endocrine system, is stimulated and becomes more active in its function. It likewise stimulates all the major endocrine glands throughout the body and increases their activity and function. In the ancient systems, the duodenal area within the digestive system is considered part of the endocrine system. It is quite common for meditators to experience an increased activation in this area and develop digestive disturbances until they have cleared the associated blockages and integrated the fullness of glandular function.

Since being with Muktananda was a constant meditation in terms of his enlightening entrainment, I, too, manifested this process of digestive disturbance and was quite physically sick for some time. To assist the process, Muktananda instructed me to follow a very strict diet. He told me to eat only milk and chappatis (an Indian flat bread made daily for each meal) three times a day and nothing else. I could have as much as I wanted, but only three times per day: breakfast, lunch, and dinner.

I followed his instructions, and this diet gradually began to cure my digestive distress, but another problem appeared simultaneously. I began to have regular nightly nocturnal emissions. This did not fit with my database about puritanical sexual celibacy, and I became obsessively concerned and stressed over it. I finally reasoned that this was due to all the milk protein, and I decided to change to soy milk instead of cow's milk. I did not ask Muktananda because I was too embarrassed about the sexual issue, and I convinced myself that he had only said to drink milk, and whether it was vegetable or animal milk would not matter. My plan worked, the nocturnal emissions ceased, and I was content within the maintenance of my limited sexual database.

Then, one day Muktananda was in the kitchen and discovered the soy milk that was kept for me. The drama intensified. He called me to his quarters and wanted to know why I had switched to soy milk, saying that I was obviously some kind of fool if I could not even follow his simple instructions. I finally confessed about the nocturnal emissions and my confused data about celibacy, and his response was radically liberating. He said that he had instructed me to drink the milk because he wanted to increase the production of seminal fluid. When the body is constantly within an enriched environment of decelerated enlightening frequency, it quickly consumes its reservoir of available nutrients and then progresses to a sort of malnutrition. A major symptom is digestive distress, which is an alarm that signals the need for increased nourishment. The ultimate nourishment is seminal fluid, from which the most subtle energy is extracted and restores the depleted reservoir. After the subtle energy has been extracted, the waste as gross seminal fluid is discarded. The nocturnal emission is the natural process of discarding the waste so that more seminal fluid can be produced. It is a meditative, enlightening process and has nothing whatsoever to do with sexual celibacy. He insisted that I return to the cow's milk and continue until further notice. I remained on this diet for one full year before he let me relinquish it. Not only did it clear my blockages and enable more blissful expansions in awareness, it also radically shifted my limited data about sexuality in general and my specific data with regard to celibacy.

So what about Muktananda and his sexual expressions? It is always nondual versus dual awareness that spells the ultimate liberation. When you have moved beyond ego limitation and become constant in unity awareness, there is no other. There is only the play of one consciousness, and everyone is a reflection of yourself. Everyone is a reverberation of the same truthful love. Where then is relativity? Where is there anyone separate from yourself with whom you could relate? In such a state of being, relationship is an illusion. Muktananda was truly celibate insofar as true celibacy is the experience of no other. True celibacy is a state of unity awareness.

When Muktananda taught us to practice celibacy, he was teaching us to expand awareness from the dual to the nondual. The gateway of sexual expression in all its multidimensionality has always been used as a meditative technique to deliver progressive unity awareness. Muktananda was certainly within the Tantric tradition, which has always validated the appropriateness of meditative sexual expression. Many of those who were intimate with Muktananda described it in the same way. They said that there was nothing "sexual" about it. It was the most beautifully meditative experience of oneness and Source that they had ever experienced, and it culminated in the most sublime state of unconditional love and unity awareness they had ever known. Through its experience, they accessed states of self-acceptance and self-love that only mystics have ever touched, and in the fullness of pure love they tasted absolute freedom and transformed themselves forever.

But, what of Muktananda? What did he experience? Since for him there was no other, he simply experienced himself as Source. The truthful love he lived was reflected back to him in equal abundance. His equilibrated state never changed. Rather, he merely celebrated Sourceful human existence in all its magnificence and flowed with whatever was spontaneously happening, be it sexual or otherwise. If we are ever truly free, our freedom must include the fullness of all our human expressions. We cannot single out sexual expression and set it aside, limited and bound, believing that it is other than Source. If we are truly free, we celebrate life as one consciousness, a unity in diversity, and that includes human sexuality. Muktananda was truly free. He accepted everything as Source. He played as consciousness itself. He celebrated the eternal unity awareness of all that is. His demonstration was liberation.

As for myself, I have journeyed a fullness of sexual expression throughout my life. In my present awareness, I am a true celibate as I have relinquished the illusion of another. My experience has been multisexual, and I have explored the many dimensions of human sexual expression. Since everything is the diversification of one unity, limited identifications and comparative classifications, such as heterosexual, homosexual, bisexual, self-sexual, or asexual, with one judged better than another, are absolutely fraudulent.

A human being is a multisexual being and contains the possibility of all sexual expressions simultaneously within itself. In any moment, we can express any of them. If we relinquish dualistic judgments, we are simply whatever we are. I have enjoyed the celebration of intimate sexual expression with whatever form presented itself as a reflection of myself in the moment. In this moment, I can truthfully say that I experience no other. I shall remain a celibate within the truthful reality of no other; yet within the freedom of nondual awareness, if an intimate journey of reflection ever presents itself in my world, I shall experience it as appropriate no matter in what form it manifests. I shall continue to celebrate my unity in all its diversity. I shall continue to love myself as I am, as all and everything, as Muktananda so truthfully demonstrated to me in his dance of love, sex, and Source. His living example was so free, manifesting real purity, the freedom from all limitation.

No wonder the Vedic tradition demands our attention with the statement: "A true enlightening master is absolutely free." This for me is the mastery of being human. Again, it is the bliss of freedom.

CHAPTER 12

Experiencing True Love

If two lovers surrender to each other,
they merge into the bliss of love.
But if they both remain in their own egos,
it's mutual usury, and illusion is perpetuated.
Relationship is about union.
When two disappear, one alone is.
MASTER CHARLES

In the dance of Source as love, what exactly is true love? How does one experience it? In my present awareness, it is really very simple, but egos and minds make it complex. Yes, it's all a game for the fun of it, entertaining and appropriate in all its madness, but until one is fully aware, the journey is arduous and stressful, full of bumps and blocks, trials and tribulations, suffering and misery. Sometimes the process seems relentless, but still we pursue it: love, the be-all and end-all of life. With it we are more alive; without it life is just a boring charade. Everyone is looking for love. The confusion is that we perpetually look outside of ourselves and become intricately entangled in dualistic love, which is never what it is supposed to be. We are always the subject of someone as an object, and our experience is most often gnawingly lacking, never quite enough, and endlessly unfulfilling. Truthfully, real love is nondual, and the way out is in. It is always available at the center of our being in its fullness as Source. To experience it, we have to begin with ourselves. If you have never loved yourself, how is it possible to love someone else? True love is not relative. It does not exist for the sake of someone or something in addition to ourselves. It is free and independent. It is the nature of Source. We must begin with loving ourselves. This is the journey of self-acceptance, and it takes us to the center of our being, to Source as pure love itself.

Many times people would ask Muktananda how they could love him more in order to be closer to him. His response was always the same: "If you want to love me, you must first love yourself." He would say that he taught people to love themselves, that he had not learned to love another, and that it was not in his philosophy of life. What he meant was that if people were constantly balanced in awareness of Source, their energetic reverberation became a Love-field, and everyone was entrained to its blissful frequency. Within such a Love-field, self-acceptance is spontaneous, for it is beyond the ego-mind. What happens naturally is that you quite literally fall in love with yourself. Muktananda did not teach with mere words; rather, his teaching was his energetic demonstration, his constant Love-field, an entrainment within which you shifted to the center of your being and merged with the love that was your true nature. This is the ultimate in self-acceptance, and true love is about acceptance.

When I first came to Muktananda, I did not love myself. I did not yet recognize, through awareness, that I, that verily all and everything, was love itself. For me, and most human beings, love was a commodity to be acquired and possessed. The conditioned model is dualistic. One must find love and maintain it to be happy. If love is dualistic, however, it is full of fear. Fear is the possibility of the loss of love, the loss of what you possess that you believe insures your happiness, the loss of the other. Therefore, from the ego level, all steps are taken to insure the security of love, even fraudulent compromise.

In dualistic love, we live with a simultaneous fear. We say we act out of love, but really we act out of fear and pretend it is love. Fear is the culprit that makes dualistic love conditional. It is the weapon of the ego. The remedy is to relinquish the entangled confusions within our database and our ego attachment to their memory. As always, the basic principles within the Creation Game remain the same. Through so many situations, we are addressing the same truth. Pure love always dwells at the center of our being, and our access point is through self-acceptance, which is yet another form of meditation.

We can each remember our first experience of dualistic love. Mine, I am sure, was similar to most everyone else's. I can still see those steamy windows from inside the car as I passionately explored my first beloved's physical magnificence. I was all of sixteen years old, but I was head over heels in love. It just seemed to happen when I least expected it. She was a beautiful girl, and we had been friends for some time. We were irresistibly physically attracted to each other. This became the initial focus through which we found a further compatibility in our respective software programs. When the focus deepened and our data aligned, we relaxed enough with each other to manifest our first physical intimacy. In the process, we exploded into the ecstasy of love. Everything dissolved into this blissful, all-consuming fulfillment. We were high on love, beyond the ego-mind, overwhelmed with a rapture beyond our control.

I have never understood why people call it "falling in love." To me, it should be "rising in love." Perhaps it is because the loss of control through natural surrender feels like falling. But falling is down, and rising is up. Love, true love, pure love, is always an up, an affirmation of life. We were high on love, high on life. We could not get enough of each other, and being conditioned to believe that the experience of love was because of the other person, we found every possible way to be together constantly. Whenever we could manifest it, we were intimately entwined, bees to the flower, drunk on the intoxicating nectar of love.

I had never been that attentive with anyone. The intrigue of intimacy was an overwhelming magnet. It demanded an ever-narrowing focus, and therein lies the mystery. It is a natural form of meditation. Whenever we manifest another as a powerful enough focus, we experience an equilibration in being, and through expansion of awareness, transcend the dual illusion. Subject and object merge, and pure awareness as love expresses itself. We become blissful, high, and intoxicated with love through our full attentiveness to the moment. Perhaps for the first time, we are fully present and alive here and now. This is basic meditative technique as applied to the experience of falling in love. As long as the focus endures, the balance remains, and pure love flows spontaneously. It fills us completely, and nothing additional is required. We need neither to eat nor sleep; the fullness of love is enough. Yet, in our conditioned confusion, we believe that love comes from the other person, and we become obsessed with possession. We manipulate everything to insure that the beloved is forever ours and that love will be preserved.

This was the case with my first love. We were together all the time, maintaining our nondual focus, merged in love. For three months, we could not get enough of each other. We stole away on the weekends, lying to our parents about what we were really doing, and spent all our time in some hotel room celebrating the sexual intimacy of our love. Food was not a consideration, nor was sleep, unless it was entwined in each other's arms, a short rest before further sexual expression. Even then, it was a conscious kind of sleep, for pure love had made us so attentive that deep sleep was unnecessary. We were constantly in each other's awareness, and the experience we shared seemed to give life meaning. But we did not think of meanings and definitions; rather, we abandoned the mind and remained somewhere beyond it in a peaceful stillness saturated with blissful love. Suspended in the fullness of the moment, everything was perfect.

Then our individual situations changed, and life continued its flowing and diversified intensity. She went away to boarding school, and I died a slow and silent death. We tried to continue our mutual possession, but the circumstances made it impossible. The spaces between our intimate opportunities lengthened, and the flowers withered upon the vines. Before too long, she found another with whom to manifest a focus, and we were finished. It was an agonizing separation, the pain and disappointment almost more than I could bear, for love was gone, and no matter how I tried, I could not get it back. Where there had been the blissful high of pure love, that all-consuming celebration in every cell of my being, there was now just a miserable emptiness, and I was alone and rejected. Where there had been life, there was now just death in all its gloomy desperation. Alone in my room, I wept silently, in mourning for the loss of love.

In the depths of my depression, a familiar stillness slowly emerged. As I detached from the dualism of my suffering in retreat from the intensity of the pain, I became naturally meditative once again. It was night and in the quietude of my darkened room, the Divine Mother, in all her luminous radiance, appeared again at the foot of my bed. The peace of Source entranced me, and my misery vanished into the saturating nurturance of her presence. Through the ecstasy of her being, she comforted me with motherly love and told me that I had to experience this journey in all its intensity. It was appropriate, and one day I would understand why it was necessary. But for now I must simply endure and know that she was always with me, watching from a distance. Her stillness blanketed me with a quiet sense of comfort, and the pain dissolved into the bliss of oneness. I fell asleep at the ever-fulfilling bosom of the loving Mother.

My journey continued, and over the next few years before meeting Muktananda, I explored a variety of dualistic relationships. Two more were as deeply loving as the first, and yet, they all seemed to tell the same story in the end: of focus diminished, balance forfeited, and Sourceful love lost. I endured the experience, encouraged by the comforting reminders of appropriateness that I received every now and again from the Divine Mother in the darkened stillness of my bedroom. I learned more from each progressive experience of what love was all about.

Love is a progression from the dual to the nondual, from the fragmentation of imbalance to the wholeness of balance. As human beings, we are conditioned in dualistic love, and when the nondual focus within a relationship fragments and through imbalance love is lost, we return to the familiar model. We project love onto the other person, and there follows the stress of possession, condition, manipulation, comparison, and judgment. This is the ego level of love. It is a memorized pattern with which we are identified. It is limited, and so is the love that we manifest with it, a love that is fragmented and lacks consistency.

Most people who say that they have love are not living love. They are not as constantly high on love as they were when it first happened. Rather, they have gradually contracted their awareness and pure love has eroded. They are only living their confused ego-based memory of love. Their love has become a lie because repetition is stagnant and devoid of the creativity of Source. It is never the same as the pure love beyond the ego-based memory that they repeat daily. Perhaps this is why the divorce rates are over 75 percent. Most marriages are a lie. Something is always missing and seems to diminish more with each passing day.

We unconsciously try everything we know to restore the original love, looking at everything as outside of ourselves. This never works, because love is energy. It is consciousness. It is awareness. All that we do cannot insure its perpetuation, because all our efforts are stressful and lead to dualistic imbalance, which proportionately limits awareness. Then, in our frustration, we are left with fear as the reflection of our lack of love—fear, which is only the reflection of our self-negation. The bottom line is that we do not love ourselves.

Most people try to love another without having mastered or even explored loving themselves. This is a bit like trying to sing an opera when you have never studied music. You would probably sound hideous. But this is what most people do with love, and their relationships and marriages are just hideous facades for what they know deep within themselves is really missing: love, the real love, the pure, all-consuming love beyond ego. Yet, if a powerful enough balancing focus manifests with another and pure love explodes again beyond ego, you will always surrender to it until eventually you master the game and discover that pure love is your very nature, that true love is loving yourself beyond all definition, and that the more you try to understand it and create systems to secure it, the more it evades you.

The love that you seek is the love that you are. There is a beautiful story that illustrates this truth: A lover came to the beloved's door and knocked. A voice from within whispered, "Who is there?" And the lover answered, "It is I." Then the voice said, "There is no room in this house for thee and me," and the door was not opened. So the lover went back into the desert and fasted and prayed and meditated. At the end of a year, the lover returned to the beloved's door and knocked. And the voice from within asked, "Who is there?" This time the lover, having moved beyond the illusion of duality, answered, "It is thyself," and the door was opened.

Whenever you move beyond the dualism of the ego-mind and touch the center of your being, you will always experience love. It is the nature of Source. Love has never gone anywhere. You have come and gone in your mind. Love is not an object to be possessed, but an expression of true being. As Muktananda often said, "When God's love exploded, this universe came into being. As this Sourceful love began to pulsate, we and all beings came into being. So we live as love, in love, for love, and seek only love." For love is all there is, and loving yourself is simply living love.

CHAPTER 13

Living Only Love

Embracing lovers have their eyes closed.
They revel in the love within
in that moment.
Love is always inside
and is easily experienced if you look within.
MUKTANANDA

Muktananda was constantly living love, for he had mastered self-acceptance. He first had loved himself, and thereafter it was inevitable that all around him reflected the same nondual love back to him. He was constantly basking in the blissful, inebriating ecstasy of pure love. It had become his eternal expression, as was unconditionally demonstrated in the consistency of his powerful Lovefield. He was stress free and fearless, anchored in the awareness of himself and his world as the embodied expression of true love.

Once, shortly after I had become his personal secretary, Muktananda and company were on tour in Los Angeles. We were staying at a ranch retreat about an hour north of the city. Muktananda was scheduled to present an evening

program in central Los Angeles, and since his regular driver and his car were still in transit from the previous city,
I was asked to drive him to the program. Someone had
loaned a car for his use, and I was to drive him in it. It was
a two-seater Mercedes with a very small backseat. I assumed that the translator would travel with us since I
could hardly understand Muktananda's language. It had
been raining heavily the whole day, and the rain continued as we were to depart. I pulled the car up the inclined
driveway next to his quarters at the appointed time, and
his attendant opened the door. Muktananda got in, but
there was no translator. I was informed that the translator
had gone ahead to the program and just Muktananda and
I would be in the car.

I became immediately attentive, for I had never before
been completely alone with him, and there was no translator. Also, it was pouring rain, and the driving was more
challenging than usual. To say that he became my total
focus is an understatement. As we drove along in the rain,
I had the defroster on full blast because the windows were
fogging, and it was difficult to see the road very far in the
distance. Wanting to be impeccable, as always, I was overly
alert. After about fifteen minutes, Muktananda spoke to
me as if I could understand what he was saying. Of course,
I could not make out at all what he was trying to communicate. It sounded something like "Grumm . . . grumm!" I
became even more intensely focused and attentive and
simply gave him a perplexed facial expression.

A few more minutes went by, and I assumed that what
he wanted to say was unimportant and began to relax a little, when he again repeated the same sounds. This time,
however, he also began to fiddle with the various control

knobs on the dashboard. I became really attentive. Finally, he remembered the word he wanted in English and said very loudly, "Grumm . . . grumm . . . hot . . . too hot!" The real word in the dialect of Hindi that he spoke was *garam*, which means "hot," but I had absolutely no idea what it meant. He finally retrieved the English word and was able to communicate what he wanted. I quickly turned down the temperature of the defroster and cracked the windows just enough so that it would cool the car without flooding us with the rain. He was pleased, but I had another challenge to address as the windshield now fogged over completely. I had to keep wiping it with my hand for the rest of the hour-long drive. I was so focused and attentive on driving and on him sitting so close next to me that I seemed to enter a time warp, and before I knew it we had magically arrived at our destination. Someone met the car, and Muktananda exited into the program.

With tremendous relief, I parked the car, thankful that I had managed somewhat appropriately in the situation. I was also secure that on the way back the translator would ride with us, and there would be nothing more than the driving to concern me. I went into the program hall and waited in the rear reception room while Muktananda delivered his presentation. I sat in a chair to relax a little, but immediately noticed that I was hallucinating. The longer I sat, the more the hallucination intensified until everything was disappearing and reappearing, myriad forms all dissolving one into the other. My awareness expanded to witness consciousness, and a powerful energy suddenly surged throughout my body, followed by a rush of heat that left me sweating profusely. Saturated with a peaceful ecstasy, I watched as the energy burst through my heart and gushed outward in all directions. Love flourished within this dynamic explosion, and with an effortless surrender I became love itself. It was pure, unconditional, nondual love, a love of myself, a total acceptance that encompassed everything with its intoxicating bliss. I was high on love for the sake of love. There was no other. Subject and object had merged, and pure love alone remained in all its delighting fullness, one existence eternally celebrating itself as love and love alone.

The intensity of the experience diminished enough for me to be somewhat functional by the time Muktananda had finished his presentation and it was time to drive him back to the retreat. I remained in witness consciousness and was very intoxicated with love as I pulled the car around and waited for him and the translator. The door opened, and Muktananda got in as the translator told me that he would be remaining for a while and that I should proceed to drive Muktananda back without him. As the door closed and we were alone again, my eyes overflowed with tears, for I instantly realized that we had merged into the same state of loving awareness. It was full and in want of nothing. We drove the hour-long trip in silence, sharing a love that was beyond anything I had ever experienced. This was no ordinary love. It was nondual, free, and unconditional, an elevated purity that brought bliss to the totality of my being. We had become true love itself. We were one and free.

We reached the ranch, and I drove up to Muktananda's quarters. It was still raining lightly, and the attendant wanted me to pull close to the porch so that Muktananda would not get wet when he got out of the car. The inclined dirt driveway was very muddy from all the rain and very slippery, and the car slid around as I tried to position it close to the porch. The attendant told me to back down and out and try again. I was so drunk on love that I really didn't care and just did what he asked. As I started to pull forward again, I accelerated quickly so that the momentum would compensate for the slippery mud and I would be able to get close to the porch.

With the sudden acceleration, however, the car slid to the right and went straight for the corner post of the porch. I was sure that we were going to hit it and so was the attendant, who jumped out of the way, when all of a sudden and quite magically, the car steered itself and, just missing the post, positioned itself perfectly next to the porch. Just before he got out of the car, Muktananda turned to me with a little chuckle and winked in mystical amusement. Every cell in my being laughed simultaneously.

I went to my room next to his, and as I sat on my bed I again exploded into the fullness of Sourceful love. I was so inebriated that nothing mattered. I was high on love, the love of myself as Source, and it was enough. I bent over to untie my shoes and disappeared into the unmanifest. Throughout the night, I remained merged in the absolute love of the one without a second. I emerged in the morning, lying fully clothed upon the bed, and through a hallowed haze of shimmering consciousness, saturated with the luminosity of true love, I was nevermore to be the same. I had surrendered to myself. I had become love. I was all that is.

Muktananda loved everyone unconditionally because true love is unconditional and he was anchored in this nondual state of being. The powerful vibration of this stress-free state provided a constant focus for anyone who was close to him. It seemed he transformed everyone, but really they transformed themselves when they merged with his Love-field, and all their illusory inadequacies disappeared, only to be replaced by the fullness of a seemingly radical self-acceptance. Because he fully accepted himself in all his diversity, Muktananda likewise accepted all people, no matter their background. Fools, criminals, frauds, the hurt, the wounded, the abused, and even the psychotic—they all came to a flowering through the gateway of his unconditional love and acceptance. He loved everyone as he loved himself, reflections of the equality of Source, the manifestations of love itself.

It is said that if you transform yourself, you simultaneously transform your world. It becomes a reflection of what you truly are, as love and love alone. So it was with Muktananda. He and his world were simply embodiments of pure love filled with intoxicating bliss and forever radiant in their truthful oneness. Ultimately, the same love shines through all eyes and animates all forms. If you are aware of true love, you see it reflected in all and everything.

When I first became Muktananda's personal secretary, I was awkward in the job. It was really strange to be so close to the one whom I held in such high regard. I was insecure in myself and full of doubts about my adequacy within the situation. I did not know how to be in this new context. I had no similar experience in my memory banks to repeat. However, the fear of not knowing how to be increased my attention to the moment at hand. I was stressfully alert and presented an uncomfortable demeanor beneath the facade of perfection I tried to project. I was imbalanced and filled with tension. Muktananda never directly commented on my noticeable lack of self-acceptance and self-love. He simply let me be the way I was and enveloped me with his constantly loving presence. Because Muktananda loved himself unconditionally, he accepted everyone's diversity from the detached observation of his unity. There was no stress in his environment, and everyone progressively relaxed and released in proximity to him. Before you knew it, you found yourself reverberating with love, and within such an experience self-acceptance was natural and effortless. In every way, he surrounded you with love and watched as you flowered in the expansion of true awareness.

Muktananda was a monk, and if his head wasn't shaved, his hair was always closely cropped. When the weather was cool, he wore a knit hat. This was traditional within his order of monks in India, yet in the West it stood out as different and attracted a lot of attention. His saffron robes and orange ski hat, along with his sunglasses and dark Indian skin, made him look more like a jazz musician than a religious mystic. The hats became a sort of trademark, and people loved him the more for wearing them, so they constantly gave him hats in this style as gifts. Sometimes they would buy them, and sometimes they would knit them specifically for him, all in varying shades of saffron orange, red, yellow, and even purple magenta. Because he received so many hats, it became his custom to give them away after he wore them for a while. This was considered a very special gift because it carried his energy reverberation, and people would treasure these hats and wear them while meditating or whenever they wanted to increase their Sourceful focus. Over the years of our close association, he gave me many articles of his personal clothing, including several hats, which I still treasure to this day. Most people, however, would be lucky to get even one such personal item.

During the time after I had just become his personal secretary and was still awkward in the job, he chose a truly appropriate moment to present me with my first hat. I had always wanted one and was secretly jealous when anyone else would get one, but I never asked, as it was inappropriate protocol. I had a treasured hat that I had acquired in Pakistan on the way to meeting Muktananda, but I dearly loved it and was so attached to it that I could not even consider giving it to him. It was a beautiful beaded hat that is worn under a turban by the men of that culture. It was saffron and many varying shades of white and orange mixed together. It was truly beautiful and would have looked superb on him. As the months passed and I expanded in self-acceptance and love, I wanted to express my gratitude and this perfect love in a perfect way. I finally decided to give him the possession that I loved the most to exemplify how much love I was experiencing and how thankful I was for all that he shared with me. I decided to buy nine knit ski hats and give him one a day, until the tenth and final day, when I would present him with the most special beaded hat that I loved so much.

For nine days, I dutifully and with great love presented the hats to him in the daily public programs. At the end of the program, he would sit and greet people before leaving. A line would form and one by one people would come forward to receive his blessing. It was traditional to give him a gift of fruit or flowers or whatever you felt was appropriate. Each day he became more amused as I presented him with yet another hat. He would laugh and pat me on the head and in some subtle way acknowledge that he was aware of my intention. On the tenth day, I presented him with the special hat, which I had wrapped in a beautiful piece of silk cloth. He unwrapped it with careful attention, like a child receiving a mysterious gift, and upon viewing it verbally exclaimed on its beauty. Then, with a gesture to validate the love within my intention, he removed the hat he was wearing and put this new one on his head. It looked so spectacular glistening in the light that everyone in the room applauded. I was flooded with joy at the bliss of expressing love for him in a way that meant so much to me, and I was wonderfully content in the moment.

I stood up from kneeling in front of his seat and slowly started to walk away, when he called me back. He told me to sit for a moment and gave his attendant some instructions. The attendant returned with something wrapped in a piece of silk cloth and gave it to Muktananda. He unwrapped it and revealed that it was one of his favorite meditation hats. It was different from those he wore in public, a kind of a close-fitting skull cap intricately crocheted into a unique pattern. However, it was not saffron orange, but shades of dark plum and lavender, which have always been my favorite colors. He pulled me to him, placed this hat upon my head, patted me several times, and told me to wear it for meditation, as he had worn it for a long time and it was full of pure love. Then he added, "Always remember, what you give is what you get. If you sow the seeds of love, you will always reap a harvest of love. Let this hat be a symbol of the ever-expanding love of yourself as Source."

Tears filled my eyes in the beauty of the moment, and Muktananda pulled me onto his lap and embraced me with even more love. Then he dismissed me, and I left the program and returned to my room. I sat on my bed and drifted into a deep transcendental state of awareness. The whole of my being was saturated with unconditional love for myself as all and everything. I was delighting in the fullness of the unconditional expression of pure love. After a few hours in this state beyond compare, I emerged only to open my eyes and see the play of one consciousness dancing before me. Everywhere, scintillating, diamondlike particles bathed in a rose-colored hue shimmered and delighted within the ecstasy of their existence. There was love and love alone as each particle reverberated a purity that seemed to echo through all eternity, saying, "Love is all there is . . . there is only love . . . only love . . . only love unto forever and ever . . ." I watched, enraptured in this elevated state, until it slowly diminished, and I returned to my normal awareness. I sat quietly for a long time within the lingering reverberation of true love. I was in awe of its perfection.

Through such experiences, day after day, I was learning to love myself, and Muktananda was indeed showing me the way. He was so anchored in nondual Source awareness that the dual illusion was permanently erased. He was fearless and free in oneness—the experience of no other—and this absence of fear allowed the expression of pure love to permeate the fullness of his environment. All present relaxed as truth enveloped them and unconditional love saturated their being. Even the whole of nature responded to this reverberation. The gardens grew more lush, the fruit trees produced bigger and more abundant harvests, and the weather patterns harmonized themselves to deliver a mixture of balanced perfection. The animals, too, were entrained into this synchrony. I had read how saints like Francis of Assisi attracted all the animals and regarded them as brothers and sisters of the one. Animals were drawn to Saint Francis because his energy field radiated such love and nonviolence that they had no fear and thus approached him with full trust.

With Muktananda, I experienced the magical touch of the enlightening master with animals firsthand. Years before I had met him, Muktananda had been given a baby male elephant. Within his tradition, this was a very auspicious symbol, and he had raised this elephant with great love. Years later, when the elephant matured, Muktananda was away for long periods of time in foreign countries. It so happened that just as we were about to return to India from a two-year absence, the elephant experienced his first rut. News came that he was uncontrollable and acting very irrationally, with continual trumpeting and attempts to break out of his quarters. Muktananda instructed the animal caretakers to contain the elephant as best they could until he returned in a few days' time. When we finally did return, the elephant was fully into his passionate madness and had to be chained in his quarters lest he would break loose and terrorize the countryside. His trainer-attendant could not manage him at all and feared going too close since the trunk could be a very dangerous weapon. Everyone was very nervous and concerned and kept a safe distance from the elephant's raging intensity.

For a day or two, Muktananda simply remained in his quarters and let his enlightening reverberation permeate the environment. Then he went to visit the lustfully mad elephant. He had a chair placed just out of the elephant's reach and sat silently upon it, filling the whole space with peace and love. Every once in a while he would call the elephant's name in a soft and gentle voice, and the elephant would tilt his head and focus his eyes upon Muktananda. Slowly but surely, the elephant became quiet, and Muktananda moved his chair closer, continuing the same process. This persisted over a few days until finally he walked right up to the elephant, stroked his trunk, caressed his whole body, and fed him from his hand. Everyone watched in silent amazement while this raging elephant became as docile as a newborn baby. Within a few days, he was unchained and perfectly manageable and was brought daily to Muktananda's courtyard to greet him and be fed sweets. He became translucent with the energy of Source, and his aura was visibly expanded in all directions. He, too, had merged in Muktananda's Source-field and was elevated in pure love. I observed this same phenomenon over many years with all kinds of animals, from dogs, cats, and birds to cows, deer, and snakes—all responding in the same way. In the absence of fear, love alone is, and all are attracted to it. Everything expands in nondual awareness. Everything merges with Sourceful love.

More important for us, human beings also respond to true Sourceful love. Over the years with Muktananda, I witnessed thousands of people experience radical transformations as their hearts opened within his Love-field and they tasted pure freedom. Muktananda beautifully expressed the truth of Sourceful love once in a program dialogue as he paraphrased the words of Emmet Fox. I wrote his words down then, and repeat them here in all their splendor: "There is no limitation that Sourceful love will not remove; no difficulty that true love will not conquer; no disease that enough love will not heal; no door that real love will not open. It makes no difference how deep the trouble, how hopeless the outlook, how muddled the tangle, how great the mistake; Sourceful love dissolves all into itself. If only you could be aware of the love that you are, you would be the most blissful being in the world."

In so many ways over the years of our close association, Muktananda demonstrated his freedom with regard to love, sex, and Source. He never failed to catalyze in me an ever-expanding freedom through awareness. He taught me that real human mastery includes the full celebration of all our human expressions as the play of one consciousness, and that this Sourceful celebration exemplifies a true and enduring freedom.

Another time with Muktananda, I became the focus of some rather intense negative criticism. He could easily see that I had become identified with the criticism and was suffering as a result. He spoke to me privately, saying, "What difference does it make whether they throw stones or flowers, as long as you love yourself? Love is the nature of Source. If you love yourself and your world as Source, you are forever free."

A story that I like very much delivers the point. There was once a famous artist who was also quite enlightening in his awareness. He had just completed a new painting, and it was displayed publicly. It was a nature scene of a serene garden. In the center of the garden was a door. The critics came to review this painting, and with egotistical judgment, one of them said to him, "This is a beautiful painting. Your technique is impeccable. But, we have found one mistake. You forgot to put a handle on the door!" The artist smiled in an enlightening way and very peacefully replied, "This is the door to the human heart. It can only be opened from within."

It has been many years since with Muktananda's assistance I first opened the door to my truthful heart from within and experienced the absolute love at the core of my being. I continue to delight in its eternal and unconditional flowering. In these moments, I live in the full acceptance of myself and my world as Source. I am blissful, peaceful, and radiant with love. I am free in the totality of the one love that is all and everything. It shines through all eyes, and it reverberates in all forms. From the Source of my being, its eternal truth is ever-resounding. I love myself as I am, for I am all that is. With this truthful awareness, I celebrate the bliss of freedom.

PART FIVE

FREEDOM

I meditate
There is stillness
The one is revealed
Indigo blue
Iridescent and scintillating
Bliss merges into bliss
And flows through the quantum portal
Beyond the beyond
Light dissolves
Creation disappears
Pure awareness is
One Source
I am, but there is no me
Freedom unto forever and ever
Ah, the bliss, the incredible bliss,
Of freedom

CHAPTER 14

Monastic Initiation

There is a difference between happiness and bliss.
Happiness is when you win the lottery,
get a new car, or someone pays you a compliment.
Bliss is when you do not need any of these to be happy.
DEEPAK CHOPRA

Dictionaries tend to supply similar definitions of freedom: It is the state of being at liberty, free and independent. It is the absence of limitation. It is the autonomy of not being controlled or influenced by outside forces. We all have so many concepts in our database about freedom. It is undoubtedly one of the most prized of human possessions. Westerners especially pride themselves on their freedom, or perhaps I should say they pride themselves on the freedom that they think they have. If human beings are influenced by the programmed mind, then according to the definitions of freedom, they are not truly free. Rather, they remain limited by their beliefs and live within the illusion of their freedom. This is not true freedom.

A true enlightening mystic, however, is absolutely free, and since all limitation is related to the mind, the mystical journey is one that culminates in mastery of the mind. It entails a progressive process of transcendence through which one becomes anchored in the Sourceful awareness that is greater than the mind and forever beyond it. This is the unitive state of nondual oneness. This is the state of balance. This is pure freedom.

It was a beautiful summer day in India as I sat contemplating freedom, and the sun rose regal, breaking the horizon and flooding the temple with morning light. The chanting session continued, and as I watched through the intoxication of meditative awareness, I was filled with a unique excitement. This was the last full day of preparation before I was to be initiated into monkhood. The following day, I would take a major step on my journey of progressive freedom and assume the vows of a renunciant. A great mystic once said, "As the banks of a river lead it unto the sea, so does discipline lead to liberation." Initiation into monkhood is a disciplined path of relinquishing superfluous mental distractions and narrowing the meditative focus, which eventually leads to transcendence of the mind. This ultimate renunciation, then, is of the mind as a limited database, and the resultant experience of Source awareness spells true freedom.

I had been with Muktananda for six years and had been diligently prepared for this special initiation. I would be among a very select and small group, which included the first of his foreign disciples to become monks in his tradition, the Vedic tradition, the most ancient lineage of renunciants in the world. It was also Muktananda's birthday celebration, and many distinguished guests would be present, including

Maharishi Mahesh Yogi of TM fame, Mahamandaleshwar Brahmananda, who would officiate for Vedic authenticity, and several senior monks, sages, and enlightening mystics in their own right. Several thousand people in all were gathered, and the ashram reverberated with celebration. I was as excited as a small child, and as I listened to the chanting, I recalled the unique unfolding of my journey that had led me to these moments.

Six years earlier, I had returned to the United States after having spent my first few months with Muktananda in India. I was preparing to join him on his forthcoming American tour, and I first needed to attend to some personal affairs so that I could be with him when he arrived. I lived as disciplined a daily life as I could, modeled on my recent stay with him, and I meditated each day as he had taught me.

One day Muktananda appeared before me in a vision within my morning meditation, and with great intensity told me to prepare to shave my head. He said that it was my destiny, and that I would understand in time. The shaven head is the symbol of monkhood for the enlightening sages of his tradition, and I was intrigued that he was suggesting this to me. As I have said, during my teenage years, I had been obsessed with following a religious vocation. I had wanted to be a monk, yet I found the monastic context within Catholicism too fraudulent, and with great struggle all the way to the door of the seminary, I finally abandoned the whole idea. I had not revealed this to Muktananda, yet now he was foretelling that my desire to become a monk would somehow come to pass in the future.

Some time later, after I had become his personal secretary, Muktananda discovered that I knew astrology, and he questioned me about it. Astrology is very respected within the Vedic tradition, and is used for calculating auspicious moments in time. I had learned astrology in my early teens. It was simply there in my memory, and with minimal refresher study I was incredibly proficient. Muktananda told me that I had retained this skill from previous human journeys, and that it was not unusual that I would still have access to it in memory. He asked me to bring his astrological chart to our next meeting. When I showed him the chart, he asked me what I saw, but before I could answer, he said, "Your chart is very similar to mine, is it not?" Certainly he did not need me to interpret astrology for him! It was just his way of making me more attentive to my destiny, which was obviously similar to his. Now it is much clearer to me than it was all those years ago in his room with the astrological charts. And indeed I have become a veritable contemporization of him.

Muktananda had journeyed to the United States, where over several tours he spent considerable time visiting various cities and, with my help and that of other American disciples, forming the beginnings of a series of meditation centers. One time before we returned to India, I was with him and one of his visiting Indian trustees in an elevator on the way to one of his program presentations. As the elevator slowed to our floor, he turned to the trustee and said, "When we return to India, I am going to make him a monk." This was his way of announcing that it was soon to be official, yet the surprise filled me with blissful excitement, and everything slowed to absolute stillness as the reverberation of Sourceful awareness encompassed the elevator. I felt a powerful sense of déjà vu, and the truth of this strange destiny felt as familiar as an old pair of shoes.

Now the day was almost at hand, and soon I would officially become a monk. I had been trained diligently under Muktananda's direct supervision by a senior Indian monk. He was classical and disciplined and set a perfect example from which to learn. The whole context was explained in detail, and I became familiar with the fullness of this ancient tradition. A thorough study of related philosophical systems was included, and blended well with my previous education in comparative religion and philosophy. To receive this special initiation from an enlightening mystic such as Muktananda was considered rare and would most definitely catalyze a radical shift in awareness. This was the focal point of the whole process. The initiation ceremony would take place over several days and culminate with Muktananda's special empowerment, or transmission of energy. As the time approached, I found myself as ready as I could be and filled with an understandable excitement.

Muktananda had been ill for a couple of months and had to be hospitalized for tests and rest in Bombay. For a while we thought that the initiation would have to be postponed, but as the time drew closer Muktananda had insisted that we proceed with the preparations. He was still recuperating when he returned to the ashram shortly before the event, but he was very determined that it should take place, and he chose to disregard his doctor's recommendations about his participation. One day before his return, I had visited Muktananda in the hospital in my secretarial capacity, assuming that he was not feeling well. I told him that I was so sorry that he was ill. He gazed at me, his eyes dilating with bliss, and told me, "I am not only this body. . . . I am the eternal witness. . . . I am consciousness. . . . I am blissful." He was so radiantly intoxicated that he demonstrated a metanormal state of being even in the midst of what the rest of us thought of as illness and suffering.

The morning chant concluded, and the final preparations for the initiation continued. During the afternoon, I had the opportunity to meet privately with Muktananda and directly express my gratitude and the fervor of my renunciation. I offered him the last of my most treasured possessions, most of which he had given me over the years, and he accepted them, acknowledging my intention. He spoke of what was to happen in the initiation, inspiring me the more. He said that he was pleased with me and that I would have a blessed future. Then he pulled me onto his lap and, stroking my back, filled me with that love that only disciples can ever experience from an authentic mystical master. Thereafter, I was allowed to kiss his feet, a rare and coveted blessing within his tradition, which was so powerful it left me reeling. I reluctantly relinquished his presence, poised and ready for the initiation at hand.

According to scriptural injunctions, the initiation ceremony for the select few of us was performed over several days by Vedic Brahmin priests. We were secluded and sequestered within the ashram cowshed, which is considered a pure and holy place. It had been prepared carefully by the priests, and there we went through the several phases of this intricate initiation into formal renunciation. On the second day, our heads were shaved. The Indian razors were less than sharp and left my head on fire with razor burns. The irritation was so intense that I wet a thin cotton towel with cold water and wrapped it around my head like a turban.

I kept it this way through the next day, and as the ceremony proceeded every so often a vision would flash before me of a man facing me wearing the same style of turban. The only difference was he was Indian, and his turban was orange. His face was very clear, and he just seemed to be watching me. As the ceremony progressed in ritual intensity, my awareness expanded, and I found myself elevated in ever-increasing bliss. We hardly slept, as we were enjoined to meditate through the night and immerse ourselves in the repetition of special Sanskrit prayers to purify us completely.

When the priests were complete with their purificatory rituals, the Mahamandaleshwar and his entourage of monks arrived to continue the ceremony and bring it to its culmination with Muktananda's final transmission of energy. The Mahamandaleshwar's name means "Lord of the Great Circle," and he is the equivalent of a cardinal in Catholicism. He is a very enlightening monk and mystical master in his own right, with many disciples. He has the authority according to Vedic tradition to officially confer monkhood.

During a break in the ritual, I was sitting near one of the monks in his entourage, and I noticed a book that he was reading. The photograph on the cover got my immediate attention, for it was the man with the turban who had appeared to me in my visions. Looking closely, I recognized him, for he was famous within the Hindu tradition. His name was Swami Vivekananda, and he was responsible for bringing the Vedic tradition to the West at the turn of the century. He was a disciple of an equally famous Indian mystical master named Ramakrishna, and their journey together had become a model of the master-disciple relationship. The stories of their journey are well known, and Muktananda often referred to them in his presentations. The moment I recognized him, his presence seemed more powerful and constant around me, and his image would not leave my awareness. I was very pleased and considered the relationship of Vivekananda to Ramakrishna an interesting comparison to my relationship with Muktananda. The contemplation took me higher. Little did I know how prophetic an omen it was.

The Mahamandaleshwar led us through the remaining rituals as we sat around a blazing fire offering our renunciation into it in synchrony with his scriptural recitations, until the ritual reached a culmination and he stopped. In the suspended silence, with the fire as a witness, he solemnly told us that this was the point of no return. If we continued, we must be absolutely sure that we could maintain this renunciation for the whole of our lives. We were afforded a moment or two for contemplation, and then each one of us was asked if we wished to continue. The ritual intensified to its conclusion and seemed to consume us in its raging flames.

Thereafter, we walked in a funeral procession, symbolic of our renunciation of unconscious life, to the nearby river. I can clearly recall standing naked in the river under the stars, screaming my renunciation of the world and affirming my commitment to a life of meditation and Source-conscious awareness. We came out of the river and were given loincloths to wear, and we were then wrapped in a simple saffron cotton cloth. After a final ritual, we proceeded to Muktananda's private quarters for the special empowerment of his energy transmission.

It was about five o'clock in the morning as one by one we met privately with Muktananda. He was seated on the master's seat as I entered. I was instructed by an assistant monk to prostrate myself before him as a symbol of the vow of obedience, and then, as I kneeled in front of him, he anointed me with sacred ash as a symbol of renunciation. Then, with great solemnity, he gave me my monastic name. I did not know what name it was to be in advance, rather opting to leave it up to him to decide on something appropriate. I was amazed when he said, "Henceforth from today, you shall be known as Swami Vivekananda Saraswati." Immediately I understood the vision of the man in the turban and its prophetic message. Rushes of enlightening energy filled my being.

Then a cloth was placed over our heads to insure absolute privacy. Holding my head in his hands, Muktananda whispered into my ear the empowering scriptural incantations. The cloth was removed, and I was anointed again with sacred ash by a senior monk. Then I was dressed in my formal saffron robes of monkhood, and when all the others were complete and assembled, Muktananda addressed us with a most inspiring talk about the potentials and possibilities of our new lives. Finally, he gave us each some sweets from his hand directly into our mouths. As I was about to move away, he stopped me and said, "You have gotten a great name!" He made this statement so lovingly that it conveyed the intimacy of our relationship of many years. Thereafter, we were dismissed to be presented to the public and then to retire to seclusion and rest.

When the public festivities were concluded, I went to my room and sat quietly for several hours, drifting and flowing within the most sublime of nonordinary states of Source awareness. Everything within my vibrational being seemed pure and different, as if washed clean of all previous impressions. I was not the same as I had been before the initiation. The experience was both real and sublime, and, indeed, in all dimensions of my being I had been reborn into a life free from superfluous distractions.

The birthday celebration continued for another week, and since Muktananda was not physically well, his participation was kept to a minimum. All business was postponed during this time. Shortly after the celebration was over and all the guests had left, he suffered a heart attack. The medical people wanted to take him back to the hospital, but it was a long trip to Bombay, and they were concerned that it would be too dangerous for him to travel so far in his condition. Also, he refused to go. He said that he wanted to remain at the ashram, and that they should tend to him there. As they continued to pressure him into going to the hospital, he called me to his quarters.

He was lying on his bed with tubes running everywhere and heart monitors beeping, yet he was as blissful as ever. He asked me what was happening in the stars. He asked me if he went to the hospital whether he would ever return to the ashram. Intuitively, I knew that he just wanted me to support his position of remaining in the ashram, so I responded that he should not go to the hospital. With many other such validations, he convinced the medical people and remained at the ashram. Over time, he recovered, but these were rather intense days for his disciples. We were not ready to relinquish his physical presence, and the very thought of it was stressful. We meditated and chanted and tried to generate as much of a Source-field around him as we could to assist in his healing. Truly, we needed it more than he did. It quieted our minds and made us peaceful. Slowly, he began to improve, and the medical people announced that he was out of physical danger but would need a long period of rest and recuperation. We relaxed, and life went on.

CHAPTER 15

Silence and Seclusion

Ordinary men despise solitude,
but masters make use of it.
Embracing aloneness,
they realize oneness with the whole universe.
LAO-TSU, TAO TE CHING

Following his illness, Muktananda remained in virtual
seclusion, seeing no one, but after about a week and a half,
he sent me a message that I should prepare to return to the
United States. This came as a complete shock and really
got my attention. I asked to see him, and after another day
or two, I was told that he would see me before I departed. I
could not believe that this was happening. I did not want
to leave him. Yet, I had accepted a vow of obedience within
the monkhood, and I was expected to be responsible to it.
Why was he sending me away? Our journey had been so
incredibly close over many years, and now everything was
going to change. I agonized in my mind over the seeming
separation, but I had to obey his command, and I proceeded to prepare for departure.

Finally, the day of my departure was at hand, and I was to leave in a few hours' time, but still he had not called me. I had been told that I would be participating in two national retreats, one in New York and one in California, but that is all I knew. About an hour before my departure, Muktananda called me to his quarters. He was lying on his bed surrounded with blue light as soft Indian classical music played in the background. I bowed as usual and sat on the floor next to his bed. Slowly, he sat up and appeared rather intensely focused within a very expansive state of Source awareness. He motioned me closer to the bedside. Then he instructed me, beginning with the words, "This is the command of the master for you." He continued speaking somewhat aphoristically, telling me that I should appear at the two retreats, but more important, that thereafter I was to go to his small ashram in Los Angeles and enter into a three-month period of absolute silence and seclusion.

He then dictated a very strict daily schedule for me to follow. He continued, saying that my awareness would unfold completely during this time and that I should keep my mind merged in Source. He spoke of Ramakrishna and Vivekananda and drew similarities with our relationship. He said that Vivekananda experienced such total illumination because his master was standing behind him with his hand on his shoulder, and that the same was true for me. He said that I would become like him.

Then he reminded me of a story. The story tells how Vivekananda begged Ramakrishna for the transmission of enlightening experience. When Ramakrishna finally conveyed the experience, Vivekananda was so overwhelmed and filled with fear that he begged Ramakrishna to withdraw it. Ramakrishna then told him that enlightening experience was based on a progressive process of purification and that the reason that he was so overwhelmed and frightened was because he was not yet clear enough to handle it. He would have to live a purificatory lifestyle of meditation and service, and then the mango of enlightening experience would be his to enjoy. Vivekananda followed Ramakrishna's instructions and ultimately experienced the fullness and constancy of enlightening awareness. His service was so vast that he was the first to educate the Western world about enlightening awareness and human mastery.

Muktananda motioned me closer to him and, with the solemnity of all his illumination, said, "Go to Los Angeles. . . . The mango awaits you there." Then, placing one hand on the back of my neck to hold my head in place, he rubbed the other hand several times around my shaven head in a circle, stopping each time at the forehead and smacking it with the palm of his hand, yet keeping a rhythm of motion that was coordinated with his voice as he repeated over and over, "My master did this to me when he sent me into silence and seclusion. . . . My master did this to me when he sent me into silence and seclusion. . . ." The energy transmission was so powerful that I reeled with Sourceful hallucination, and every cell of my being was filled with bliss. I was red hot with inner heat, as if the channels of my subtler bodies were being fried in the intensity of energetic expansion. Yet, Muktananda's love was so all-encompassing that I was not afraid and easily expanded to witness consciousness, watching the dancing luminosity of scintillating subatomic particles as they were focused through his awareness and flowed into the center of my being. When I was filled to capacity, he embraced me, and for a few moments we merged within the pure love of the moment. Then he told me not to divulge what he had told me or what had just happened to anyone. Rather, I should leave immediately and remain in silence, speaking only when necessary. So saying, he dismissed me.

The car was waiting, and I immediately departed for Bombay. Since the flight was late at night, I stayed in the home of some close Indian disciples for a few hours. I was so elevated in awareness from Muktananda's transmission that I remained in witness consciousness the whole time. I just sat on the bed watching the play of consciousness before me and reveling in the bliss that enveloped me in its abundance. Tears of love flowed from my eyes as I remembered Muktananda, and my mind remained in awe of what had just transpired. I was fulfilled and in want of nothing.

I was hardly in my body during the whole of the trip back to New York. The plane was half empty, so I reclined across several seats and drifted within the rapturous ecstasy of Source awareness. Meditation was now spontaneous, a flow that I was powerless to control. I was merged with Muktananda, like a child at the breast of its mother, and profound love filled all and everything.

My mystical experience continued through the two retreats in New York and San Francisco, and it was difficult to keep it secret because of the powerful energetic presence that surrounded me and flowed through me. Whenever I would speak or lead meditations during the retreats, the focus expanded me all the more, and everyone around me was also elevated to very expansive states of awareness.

People began to flock to me after the programs and pursue me during the breaks. I retreated to my private quarters and remained alone, elevated in the meditative awareness that was unceasing. I remained secretive and silent and never discussed what was happening to me with anyone.

One morning, as I was meditating before dawn in my room, the experience of my childhood repeated itself with even greater intensity. My body locked its position, and the energy of Source surged throughout my being. My mind was racing with thought until awareness expanded beyond it. Then I lost all volitional controls as I heard the repetition: "I am Source. . . . I am Source. . . . I am Source. . . ." I then elevated in awareness beyond the mind and entered into pure absorption, suspended beyond all manifestation for more than an hour. Slowly, my awareness contracted again, and manifestation reappeared, followed by the mind repeating its affirmation of Source.

Volitional control resumed, and my body unlocked its position, yet the blissfully hallucinating play of consciousness remained. I could not get up from bed the whole day, as the intoxication was so heavy in my body that it was impossible to move. I just lay there immobilized, drifting in the most sublime states of expanded Source awareness and love for my magnificent master.

In the middle of the California retreat, I received a letter from Muktananda. He told me that the purpose of the period of silence was for me to experience Source in its totality, but thereafter I could not remain silent. He told me that I would have to share the experience with the masses, and that I would have a truly great future. He reminded me

to remember him with his hand on my shoulder, told me
he was pleased with me, and sent me his love. I wept at
the magnitude of his watchful nurturance.

Finally, I made it to Los Angeles and prepared to enter
into silence for three months as commanded by Muktananda. Many people had followed me from the retreats, and
the ashram was full around me. I could not hide my energy
dynamic, though I never talked about it with anyone. I simply continued with my preparations for the silence. The day
I arrived in Los Angeles, there was a welcoming program,
and when it was complete, I was shown to my quarters.
When everyone left, I sat on the bed and the whole room
began to whirl and swirl around me. Before I knew it,
Muktananda's presence filled the whole space. From the
distant recesses of my being, I heard the echoing repetition: "The mango awaits you in Los Angeles. . . . This is
Los Angeles. . . . The mango awaits you here. . . . The
mango is here." This confirmation of what he had said to
me in India, a mystical reminder, filled me with ever-
expanding awe in the moment.

I prepared my room in the time remaining before the
silence was to begin. Someone had recently given me a
beautiful statue of the Virgin Mother holding the Christ
child. It was about eighteen inches tall and truly lifelike.
I still have it and treasure it to this day. I hung it on the
wall over a small altar, upon which I placed Muktananda's
slippers, along with photographs of him and other great
sages who inspired me. Every day I sat before the altar and
performed focusing rituals before my meditative sessions,
covering everything with flower petals and burning fragrant incense. I was not worshipping a statue, slippers, and
photographs, but rather using these symbolic reminders to

expand my awareness of the truth of human existence. They were reflections of myself that I celebrated with love and happiness.

The appointed day arrived, and I entered into silence, recalling the words from the Katha Upanishad: "When the mind is silent, awareness alone is." I dutifully observed the daily schedule that Muktananda had given me. I would arise at 3:00 A.M., bathe and perform rituals until 4:30 A.M., prepare for meditation with breathing techniques and mantra repetition until 5:00 A.M., and then sit for meditation until 8:00 A.M., or whenever it ended. Then breakfast and a walk until 10:30 A.M., followed by meditation preparation and meditation until 1:30 P.M. Then lunch and rest until 3:30 P.M., followed by philosophical reading and journaling, a walk, and dinner. The evening included another session of meditation preparation and meditation until I retired at 11 P.M.

With each passing day, the equilibration in my being became more precise, and as a result I became increasingly more aware and attentive. The conservation of energy from not speaking was amazing. I did not require as much sleep, and I became progressively more alert and energized. My meditations quickly deepened, and before too long I was immersed in the absolute wonder of a world silently observed. Everything was so clear and pristine, and in my seclusion I was free of distraction and more easily remained elevated in the balanced stillness of meditative awareness. This was such a profound experience that I wanted it to last forever, and I entertained fantasies of remaining silent for the rest of my life. I was in love with the fullness of each moment and totally fulfilled by this truly meditative lifestyle.

My world also reflected this joyful fulfillment. One day I was out on one of my morning walks with an assistant, and we passed a young child who was standing along the sidewalk with his mother. I walked by, and when she greeted me, I smiled and nodded in acknowledgment but indicated with my body language that I couldn't talk. The little boy turned to her and said, "Why can't he talk, Mommy? Was he bad?" I still laugh when I recall it, an appropriate reflection of Sourceful amusement.

The days passed as I became more accustomed to the state of silent awareness and, after about two weeks, as the equilibrium became constant, the most incredible experiences of a million lifetimes began to unfold. As I write of them now, I relive the awe and ecstasy of their happening.

As I sat meditating in the early morning session one day, my mind became absolutely still, and suddenly my breath was suspended and my body locked its position. I relinquished all volitional control, and my eyes opened into a state of heightened awareness, alert and attentive within the observation of the moment. A hand and an arm appeared before me and slowly moved toward my forehead. The hand held a unique, translucent, almost crystalline surgical-looking instrument, and it cut a star-shaped incision into my third-eye vortex. The whole area felt numb, as if drugged with tranquilizing medication, yet I could feel the cutting of the blade. The whole environment was saturated with the celestial sounds of tinkling glass wind chimes, an angelic chorus, and slowly strummed stringed instruments. White light was refracting and reflecting everywhere like a lightning storm on a warm summer night, and the rumbling of a gentle thunder resounded through the moment. A most sublime fragrance filled the air, a billion roses and gardenias subtly pervading this mystical miracle in the magnitude of its continued unfolding.

As the moment reached its culmination, the body connected to the hand and arm revealed itself in all its radiant effulgence. It was herself, Creator of all and everything, the feminine principle expressed as the Divine Mother with whom I had shared such an intimate journey from my earliest years. She was ecstatic and loving, beaming with delight and translucently beautiful. The whole of my being ignited with blissful love, and the peace of infinite oneness filled me. There we remained, suspended beyond all motion, still and equilibrated, the equipoise of unity and diversity in all its wonderment. Then, through the majestic magnitude of scintillating silence, thousands of flowers showered down, their white petals raining over my head and gently falling all over my body until everything was covered with their silky and fragrant loveliness. Finally, after what seemed like eons of time merged in this motionless serenity, the whole manifestation gradually disappeared, becoming progressively more translucent until it was just an all-pervasive glimmering of subtle luminosity. My eyes closed, and I merged into the transcendental unmanifest of pure awareness, the state of blissful rapture beyond all form, and there I remained for three hours until the manifest reappeared, my body unlocked its position, and I regained volitional control, breathing normally once again. I was so intoxicated with bliss and filled with awe of what I had just experienced that I simply reclined and continued witnessing the fullness that delighted before me. There was only the play of consciousness, that hallowed haze of shimmering ecstasy that filled me with its all-pervasive love. I lay there within this balanced state of being until late afternoon and then was able to rise and move about the room. My body was on fire with an electric heat, and it ached all over. My forehead, the area of the third-eye vortex, pulsed with pain, and a throbbing headache encompassed me. Yet, remaining in witness consciousness, I was blissfully intoxicated, drunk within the energy of divine presence. I sat upon my bed, and looking at the photograph of Muktananda and the statue of the Virgin Mother above it, I wept uncontrollably in gratitude and love.

The days of silence continued, and my meditations intensified in their unfolding. The pulsing pain at the third-eye vortex remained constant, and the only tranquilizing medicine was meditation. I would begin in a sitting position, and the initial progression was always the same. My mind would become absolutely still, followed by breath retention, and then the body position would lock beyond volitional control. Usually the body was then stretched into a reclining position, and great surges of primordial energy would rush upward from my navel area, through the heart vortex, the throat vortex, and into the third-eye vortex. This experience was so powerful in its intensity that it would lift my upper body into the air, adjusting its position to facilitate the movement of the energy through these channels. It was a circular, spiraling movement that seemed to clear, clean, and widen the channels and open the vortices with each more intensified thrust. I would watch, alert and attentive with eyes open, in awe of the power of this energy.

Then my body would be moved into a sitting position, and she would appear, the Divine Mother, and tend to the continuing nurturance of the surgical procedure at my third-eye vortex. She anointed this center with various salves, and soothed it with loving touch, followed by a ritual celebration in which flower petals were placed upon my head and flower garlands were wrapped around my neck and I became like a golden statue upon a pedestal within a heavenly temple surrounded with radiance. Then all would slowly disappear, to be replaced with opaque blackness, out of which a tiny iridescent blue light in the center of an equally blue triangle would appear. I was mesmerized by it and watched until it and everything dissolved into the unmanifest emptiness of pure Source awareness. There I would remain until I reemerged and the meditation ended with the unlocking of the body posture and the return to normal breathing. I would recline and drift in blissful witness consciousness, recalling what I had just experienced, until I was able to arise and move around once again.

For the next month, the same process repeated itself daily. In all three of my meditation sessions it was the same. At first, the powerful intensity of the primordial energy thrusting and surging through my body frightened me. I had no control whatsoever over it. Yet, when fear would appear, I would remember Muktananda, and the fear would dissolve in the awareness of his presence. Though I knew the philosophical context of what was happening, all my studies failed to explain the intricacies of the experience. If you have never experienced it, it is difficult to understand, and even when you have experienced it, it is next to impossible to describe fully, words failing miserably to convey the magnitude of the experience.

This is the experience of the piercing of the third-eye vortex and the opening of the crown center, wherein equilibration becomes precise and the experience of the simultaneity of unity and diversity is revealed. All the subtle body channels must be cleared to allow the unrestricted flow of the primordial energy in its fullness. When this is accomplished, balance becomes constant, and one is anchored forevermore in oneness. In the oldest mystical tradition, in Sanskrit, the third-eye vortex is called *Ajna*. It means "command." The principle is that this vortex is the seat of the mystical master, and without the master's command it cannot be pierced. The master is essential to facilitate this process to its culmination. Only true mystical masters can convey this level of transmission, for they have experienced it fully in their own journey and are adept with the intricacies required. Muktananda was obviously such a mystical master, and he was assisting me fully in this process. Without his guidance and supervision, it would have been impossible to sustain. I trusted him completely, for I knew that he had experienced all of this in its fullness and would guide me with absolute mastery.

After a month of this intensity, the channels were cleared all the way to the crown vortex. The pain at the third eye had dissipated to a lingering numbness, yet my body remained exceptionally hot from the increased flow of energy in the subtle channels. I had to move very slowly, for I was fragile in this new state, and too much activity would reactivate the throbbing headache and increase the fiery body heat. The meditation sessions remained the same in initial content, yet diversified in the later stages. For long periods of time, I would be gazing at the tiny iridescent blue light, the size of a sesame seed, which scintillated before me. This blue light is well known to mystics and is termed *Neela Bindu* in Sanskrit. It means "the blue point." It is the center of being, the Source at the core of all form. To experience it fills one with rapturous bliss, and much is revealed in witnessing it. At first it comes and goes, disappearing and reappearing, spontaneously flashing forth when one least expects it. It cannot be controlled. Progressively, it becomes more constant within inner vision and remains still and present. Ultimately, it expands in size and reveals its mystical mystery that takes one through it and beyond. It becomes the gateway to the totality of pure Source awareness. It became constant in my inner vision during these meditations and was accompanied by a stillness beyond comprehension. There was bliss and bliss alone as I observed the one Source celebrating itself before me . . . as me.

One day, in the early morning meditation, the surges of primordial energy increased in power until my whole body filled with the reverberation. I was locked beyond all volitional control and watched as the energy lifted my body into an upright position and levitated it about two feet above the floor. Then, in a slow, whirling, celebratory motion, it moved several rotations around the periphery of the whole room, a meditation in motion delighting in the demonstration of the absolute power of one Source consciousness. It was so incredible to be at the center of this experience, another witnessing of unity in diversity with its absolute abandon to ecstasy that pleasured the moment to its peak and beyond. After this joyful dance, my body was returned to its seat, and still-point meditation continued for several hours.

When you have experienced the power of Source beyond the ego-mind, there is spontaneous recognition and validation that there is but one reality, one consciousness, which empowers the totality of all that is. Then the false authority of the ego-mind quite naturally dissolves, a simple surrender to the demonstrated truth of what is.

I had now been silent for two months, and the intensity of the experience was not waning. I rarely slept at night, rather remaining a witness to the body resting and drifting into visionary states of meditative awareness. I received inner guidance during these times, and explanations of what I was experiencing, which facilitated the integration of the journey. In my waking hours between meditation sessions, I remained heavily intoxicated and radically expanded in awareness. I was high on life, and everything was beautiful. As I walked for daily exercise, the whole of nature responded with a reflection of the beauty of Source. The birds seemed to sing as an overflowing of love, a Sourceful celebration that was equally observed in every flower, every cloud, every raindrop, and every animal or human being I saw. The sun reminded me of the light at the center of my being and filled me with a radiant joy beyond compare. Indeed, I was experiencing the bliss of freedom, and every second was as divinely perfect as it could possibly be.

Once again, I was meditating in the early morning session, and the dynamic process continued with great surges of primordial energy and my body locked in the reclining position. As the jolts subsided and all was still once again, I became aware of something touching my mouth. My eyes opened involuntarily and locked, and an arm and hand were visible before me, but this time it was a man's hand. It opened my mouth and pushed its fingers inward, moving down my throat. It startled me, and I contracted my mouth, lightly biting the fingers and grabbing the arm with my hands. Then I heard a familiar laugh. It was Mukta-nanda's laugh, and the rest of his body soon appeared connected to the hand and arm. He spoke, telling me that his master had done this to him when he transmitted the totality of his energy dynamic, and now he was doing the same for me. I relaxed and the apprehension vanished as he inserted his fingers and his hand, reaching all the way to my heart. His touch there ignited a love so pure that the whole of my being exploded into enlightening ecstasy. Then, as I gazed directly into his eyes, dilated with inebriated bliss, we merged and disappeared into the emptiness beyond all manifestation. After eons of time floating in this eternal forever, I emerged into manifestation to observe myself sitting upright and gazing into the blue still point that had expanded in size to about one foot in diameter. It appeared as the balanced yin-yang symbol of Taoism and was a liquid, luminous movement contained within its balanced circumference. I watched through the numbness of bliss until it gradually dissipated, and the meditation ended in its usual way. Again, for several hours thereafter, I was absolutely still with focused awareness. I just lay there suspended in the absolute oneness of unitive consciousness.

A few days later, I was again meditating in the early morning session, sitting in the opaque darkness that commands a saturating stillness and expands awareness of Sourceful delight on the razor's edge of infinity. My body locked, and my breath was suspended within that non-dual equilibration that demanded alert attention to the moment. From this state of hallowed quietude, my eyes were thrust open and their gaze fell upon the statue of the Divine Mother on the opposite wall. The statue was iridescently luminous, as if a dim spotlight were shining upon it from above. Ever so slowly, the room filled with light, subtle yet all-pervasive, with minute diamondlike particles scintillating and dancing everywhere. Like a river flowing into the sea, the flooding luminosity increased, until soon all was aglow with divine presence, that intoxicating euphoria that catalyzes awareness and calls attention to the oneness of all that is. The hallucinogenic delight joyously overwhelmed my senses until every pore and every cell of my being was merged with the complete ecstasy of the one without a second.

All time was suspended in this holy presence, and from the conscious stillness beyond all boundaries, the celestial tinkling of a million glass wind chimes reverberated, accompanied by the trill of a lone flute, and the humming of a thousand angelic voices in harmonic chorus. Then, through this sacred serenity, a soft and echoing voice was calling my name, with a maternal magnificence that always remains beyond words, yet conveys a love that is absolute and unconditional. Finally, the form emerged from the statue, alive and expanding in size, light condensing and solidifying into shape, a three-dimensional manifestation that defies all logic, yet creates itself as spontaneously and easily as anything known to a rational mind.

It was God as Mother, the Divine Creator of universal existence who had consistently appeared since the earliest days of my youth. Now, however, she was fully animated and alive, about five feet tall, and standing in front of me. Here she was again in celebratory pose, with head tilted back to the right and arms extended upward to infinity in an expression of absolute abandon to ecstasy. Love and only love played between us, the purest love that knows no motive and is free in its unconditional oneness. Instantly, my body was moved into the reclining position, and simultaneously I became like a small child in my awareness. Then she began to play with me just as a mother plays with her child—loving, frolicking, nurturing, and delighting. She laughed as she tickled me and catalyzed me to an ecstatic giggling, and when our playful laughter filled the whole of existence, she spoke with an echoing voice, saying, "You are my child, a child of the one. . . . You are created of love. . . . You exist as love. . . . Together we are one within this love. . . . It is all that is."

She remained with me in this way, suspended beyond time, enveloping me in her radiance and saturating me with rapturous bliss. Her fragrance, roses and gardenias, permeated all space and expanded the divine intoxication. I shifted to adult awareness, and we conversed as she gently answered my questions about all these experiences I was having and what would be the outcome. She validated everything that Muktananda had told me and said that he was assisting me under her ever-watchful gaze, and that all would unfold appropriately within my destiny as she had so often told me in so many different ways. Then she concluded by saying that when I was complete in this flowering, I would merge again with her in ultimate oneness, and we would exist together forever as the love that is all and everything and forever beyond, the one without a second.

Finally, she embraced me, and as she did I became the same luminous energy that she was, and we passed through each other, a demonstration of the all-pervasive oneness that permeates the totality of forever. Ever so slowly and gradually, this radiant luminosity, refracting and reflecting itself to itself for the eternal delight of itself, diminished, condensing into the blue point that was three feet in diameter. She reappeared one last time within this iridescent orb, lifting her head heavenward and throwing her arms upward again in abandon to ecstasy, then dissolving into undulating blue light. The orb contracted into a smaller point, and then my eyes closed, revealing the same blue point within my inner vision. I watched it until I merged into the unmanifest and remained as pure Source awareness, suspended beyond time and space.

When I returned to manifest awareness, as my breath became normal and my body unlocked, I lay down and drifted within the heavy, trancelike intoxication that pervaded the whole of my being. I was too drunk to move, totally inebriated with love. I noticed the clock on the wall. Six hours had passed since the meditation began. I could not believe it had been so long, for time and space are relinquished in nondual awareness, and all sense of duration is abandoned. I was too elevated in awareness to be concerned with anything other than the play of consciousness that was so palpable within the here and now. It was enough. It was all. I remained in seclusion for the rest of the day and night, requiring neither food nor sleep, tears of love filling my eyes, floating in divine oneness and celebrating the bliss of freedom.

As the final ten days of the three months of silence were at hand, still the intensity of the experience continued. I was absorbed in a metanormal world far removed from anything that was remotely familiar. I continued to watch this divine unfolding as meditation had become a spontaneous moment-to-moment happening beyond my ability to control. There was only meditation, the unbroken awareness of Source and Source alone. My mind was absolutely still as pure oneness encompassed it. I was fulfilled as I had never been before. I was flowing within the bliss of unitive consciousness.

One week before I was to end the silence, I was sitting for my morning meditation. The progression was the same — body posture locked, breath suspended, and tremendous surges of primordial energy rushing upward to the crown of the head. My eyes suddenly rotated upward toward the crown vortex, and within its center a flashing luminosity filled my inner gaze. It was more brilliant than the light of a thousand suns, filling all space and relinquishing all darkness, a brightness beyond anything imaginable. It remained constant for a long time, bathing the whole of my being in its radiance. Then the blue point appeared within its center, iridescent and scintillating and expanding in size.

When it was about one foot in diameter, the shimmering luminosity condensed itself into the form of Muktananda. He was sitting in meditation with a blissful expression on his face. Golden light emanated from him in all directions. He was as radiant as I had ever seen him, translucent and transcendent, of the nature of light and light alone. I gazed upon this inner apparition for some time, filled with the bliss of its emanation and enraptured in the love that we shared in our oneness. Then I heard his melodic voice singing one of the mystical incantations that he loved so much. My eyes opened and locked, only to find him seated about five feet in front of me. He was absolutely real, three-dimensional in form, and as tangibly physical as I had ever seen him. He continued his singing, transforming the whole environment into pure bliss. The whole room was undulating with blue light, and love was dancing in each diamondlike particle that glistened within it.

Then Muktananda spoke, lovingly calling my name in the familiar way he had so many times during our journey together. He said that everything was appropriate and that he was very pleased with me. He indicated that the channels and vortices were now open and clear and that the stabilization would continue, demonstrated by a substantiation in nondual oneness. He told me to conclude the silence on schedule, for it was now necessary to have a period of integration, which required less intensity of manifestation. We discussed many other matters, which cannot now be revealed, and finally he said that I would soon be receiving a letter from him that would mirror all that he had just told me. Then he embraced me, pulling me onto his lap and rubbing his hand over my back as he had done so many times before, filling me with overflowing love. He reminded me that we were now one and that I was experiencing Source in its totality just as he had told me I would.

In conclusion, he fed me a divine, sweet-tasting elixir, a candylike nectar, placing it directly into my mouth. It was like pure luminous energy and instantly spread through the whole of my being, saturating all with its rapturous euphoria. Ecstatic hallucinations followed, until the whole space was filled with the light of Source delighting and dancing everywhere. Then, becoming progressively more translucent, we merged into the light and, passing through each other, became one with all and everything. All manifestation disappeared, and we dissolved into the transcendental oneness of the one without a second.

Again it was six hours before I reappeared, body unlocking and breath returning to normal. I reclined and drifted within an oceanic delight that constantly sent rushes of luminous ecstasy throughout the whole of my being. I was blissful and free. I was all that is. I remained in seclusion for the whole of the day, and later that night, alone in my room and filled to overflowing with joyful ecstasy for the resplendence of the moment, I danced, celebrating myself, celebrating my master, celebrating the Divine Mother and our oneness. Slow in motion, ecstatic in expression, tears streaming from my eyes and love delighting in every pore and cell of my being, I danced and danced as everything in me reverberated over and over again: "I am free. . . . I am free. . . . Unto forever, I am one and free."

A few days later, the silence ended. When I emerged, everyone was gathered to hear my first words in three months. I simply said, "Silence is golden. . . . It is also blue!" Being meditators, they understood exactly what I meant, and they could feel it in the reverberation of my energetic presence. Together, with great love, we celebrated my freedom.

CHAPTER 16

The Constancy of Oneness

The separation of matter and spirit is an abstraction.
The ground is always one.
PHYSICIST DAVID BOHM

Soon after my period of silence had ended, a letter indeed came from Muktananda and reiterated what he had already made known to me. He included instructions for daily meditation and added that I should remain in Los Angeles until further notice. I was so blissful it did not matter to me where I was, and I continued into the integration period that he had foretold. But now people began once more to pursue me. I could not hide my state of being, and as people shared their experience of me, the word spread and more came to see for themselves. Before I knew it, the media was at the door through someone's connection and wanted me to appear on national television. I wrote to Muktananda and told him I needed guidance. His response was to call me to India for his birthday celebration. I was ecstatic at the possibility of being with him again.

When I met him privately in India for the first time since my return, I fell at his feet and wept blissfully and uncontrollably for some time. When I was finally able to speak, heart in my mouth and tears streaming down my face, I told him that I now knew who he really was and that the illusion was forever removed that concealed his Sourceful identity. He embraced me and acknowledged our oneness with that special love that only masters and disciples ever share. He told me to remain secretive and not to reveal the details of my experience to anyone. He said that it was neither the time for the media nor for any public telling of my story, and that I should just be still and remain merged in oneness and continue the integration period.

After a few days, Muktananda called me to his private quarters and asked me to relate in detail all the experiences of the three months of silence and seclusion. He was lying on his bed surrounded with blue light, with his back toward me, listening while remaining blissfully merged with Source. After I had told him everything, he sat up and told me that all was appropriate, but that I should not reveal these experiences to anyone until he told me to do so. He added that of all his mystical experience, he had only revealed the smallest amount and this would be the same for me, for such experiences cannot be fully understood and are not for general public consumption. He embraced me and told me he was pleased with me, and then dismissed me. I was so elevated in Source awareness that I just went to my room and lay upon my bed, enjoying the glorious oneness of the moment.

People continued to pursue me, and it became difficult to remain alone and secretive. It was like trying to keep bees from a flower, and nothing really worked. I knew it would be the same when I returned to Los Angeles, and I was concerned. At the next opportunity, I discussed this with Muktananda, who told me to forget it and continue my absorption in Source awareness and everything would take care of itself.

A few days later, while doing my service of cleaning the bathroom, I slipped a disc in my back and could not move. I was taken to a solitary room, where I could rest and recuperate. The room was underneath Muktananda's quarters and adjacent to the ashram meditation room. Because you could hear through an air vent into the meditation room, you had to be silent. It was absolutely perfect. I was flat on my back, again in silence, and as close to Muktananda's Source-field as I could be. An attendant was assigned who brought me my meals, and the doctor regularly visited to check on my condition. She was also one of Muktananda's physicians and saw him several times a day. He sent me regular messages through her, unbeknownst to anyone else. The messages were always the same: that I should remain silent, secluded, and meditative as the integration period continued.

I remained in that room for two and a half months, and just as I was recovered enough to walk with a cane, it was time for Muktananda to depart for his next tour to the West. He had sent me messages that I would not be returning to Los Angeles, but would remain in India for a while. The day before he left, I saw him privately, and what he said surprised me. He again commanded me to silence and seclusion, but this time it was for a period of six months. He gave me a little cabin in the back gardens of the ashram and told me to move there after he left and continue with the daily schedule he had given me for Los Angeles. He said that this was the next phase of the enlightening unfolding, and that he would advise me further when it was completed.

The day he departed and I moved into the cabin, my back miraculously healed itself. It was as if there was never anything wrong with it at all. The doctor was amazed, but I was not, for I was aware of the magic of mystical being, and everything was delightfully appropriate. I prepared for my silence, and this time a pundit was assigned to me for daily study. He was fluent in Sanskrit and English and could directly translate deeply abstruse mystical and philosophical texts. He assisted me in a more detailed understanding of my ongoing mystical experience and connected me to a mystical history of sages and enlightening beings who substantiated the same experience. From my present state of awareness, I could understand their writings in ways that heretofore were impossible because of my lack of experience. Now all was clear, and I had joined a mystical fellowship that was vast and enduring. The pundit and I met daily for an hour and a half. He translated, and I listened. We shared beautiful moments in that little cabin. I can still see him with his long white beard, for he was eighty years old at the time, the perfect picture of an ancient mystical pundit.

The cabin was small, with just enough room for a bed, a desk, and an altar. It had an additional small room for bathing, but no running water. I had to collect the water in buckets from a nearby well each day and keep it for the next morning's bath. It was a simple renunciant's lifestyle with no frills, and I treasured every moment of it.

I entered into silence on the appointed day, and within a short time, as the silence equilibrated my being, the intensity of the meditative experience again began to unfold. My meditative progression was the same. It began with stillness of the mind, followed by the body-position lock, the suspension of breath, and the thrusts of primordial energy through the subtle channels and vortices. In every session, I would gaze upon the blue point for increasingly longer periods of time as it expanded in size and revealed more of the mystical mysteries within it. The Divine Mother, Source as Universal Creator, regularly appeared, and along with Muktananda, guided the journey with consummate precision. I was continually elevated in rapture and blissfully intoxicated in witness consciousness.

Much of what I experienced during this period must remain concealed, for it is the ultimate in the mystic's treasure and must be personally journeyed to be understood. Yet, one experience from this time conveys all that is essential, and this I share for its liberating truth.

One morning following my meditation, I opened the door to go out for a walk, and what I encountered stopped me in my tracks. Slithering down the leafy branches of a nearby tree was a large snake. It moved with such speed and alacrity that I knew it was not a mere reptile. It was conscious and aware. It circled around behind the tree and then came toward me, finally positioning itself on the other side of a stone statue that I had placed there as a reminder of the principle of unity in diversity. Daily I placed flowers there and burnt fragrant incense. Now, lifting itself up about two and a half feet, the snake opened its hood to reveal that it was a cobra, and gazed at me from over the statue. I was frozen with alert attention and dared not move. I was not afraid, for it was not a life-threatening presence, but, quite the contrary, a very expanded, Sourceful presence. The cobra conveyed a powerful awareness that pierced to the core of my being and revealed our oneness in an instant. Blue light flooded my vision, and a threefold laser beam of golden light shot directly from the cobra into my heart, third-eye, and crown vortices. Blissful elixir saturated my being and filled me to overflowing, and I reeled in the onslaught of the transmission.

As we stood there gazing into each other's eyes, the cobra's hood kaleidoscopically became a thousand hoods filling all space, and all separation instantly dissolved as we merged into the hallucinogenic oneness of the play of consciousness. We remained suspended in this state of Source awareness, as time and space stood still. It was so beautiful, I never wanted it to end. Then, ever so gradually, the intensity diminished, and the fullness of Source contracted itself into a cobra again, as it closed its hood and slowly moved away, disappearing into the surrounding jungle.

I went inside the cabin and reclined upon the bed, absorbed in bliss. I was aware that this was a most auspicious omen and portended what was soon to unfold.

The cobra is an ancient symbol in Eastern mysticism of the feminine principle, or Divine Mother. But more significant, it is always depicted in combination with its opposite, the masculine Father principle. This represents the polarization in consciousness as manifest and unmanifest, immanent and transcendent, or that perfect balance that relinquishes all duality and reveals the nondual oneness within the most subtle essence of Source. The ultimate transcendence was at hand, and I was in awe of the prophecy.

The next morning I sat for meditation, and the progression was the same. My mind became absolutely still, the body position locked, and my breath was suspended. Great thrusts of primordial energy rose upward, and my physical body rocked in its wake. My head was thrown backward, chin reaching to the sky, and my eyes pulled upward, rotating into the crown vortex. The light of a thousand suns flashed, destroying all darkness with its brilliance, a silver and gold luminosity with reflections and refractions like those of a strobe light. Then the blue triangle and the blue point within its center emerged, a scintillating iridescence of mystical manifestation, the observing of which sent pulsations of pure delight throughout the whole of my being. My tongue curled upward and pushed through the soft palate, as if in response to this magnificence, and tasted a nectar at its tip. It was a divine elixir that ecstatically excited every cell and simultaneously spread throughout my being, rendering it translucent and transcendent. Awareness radically expanded as the blue point slowly grew in size to about five feet in diameter. It was an undulating, scintillating, and reverberating mass of iridescent blue light that flooded all and everything with rapturous bliss. My eyes opened involuntarily and locked, and the outer vision exactly mirrored the inner vision and continued its unfolding.

Then the form emerged, light condensing and solidifying into shape, a three-dimensional manifestation that I immediately recognized as Muktananda, sitting in meditative posture, like a deity within a temple, eyes closed and blissfully absorbed in oneness. He slowly opened his eyes and beckoned me toward him. The blue orb expanded to include me, and we were now together within it, bathed in shimmering blue light. I bowed down before him and he placed his feet upon my head, delivering the most sacred of traditional transmissions that sent a pulsating ecstasy throughout my being. I sat upright facing him and gazing directly into his eyes as light began to form a whirlpool above his head and flow like a waterfall into him.

Then his third eye opened, and this gushing luminosity, violet and blue, a silvery indigo radiance, flowed directly into me, into my third eye, heart, and crown centers, rushing inexhaustibly until his form exploded, and there was only the shimmering light of Source. I remained within the blue orb, fully absorbed in the light, and then she appeared, the Divine and Holy Mother, the light condensing into her form standing before me in her pose of absolute abandon to ecstasy. Her fragrance permeated the hallowed light with thousands upon thousands of roses and gardenias until I was drunk with the inebriation of their olfactory delight. I bowed down and touched my third eye to her feet, and the same transmission flooded my being. Then, as I gazed into her eyes, the whirlpool of light flowed through her and into me, gushing endlessly until her form exploded, and only the brilliant light of Source remained. I again floated within the blue effulgence until my own form appeared before me in the same way—light condensing into shape until I was sitting and facing myself. The same luminous transmission flowed like a whirlpool until both forms exploded and dissolved into the blue light. I was no more as a physical form. I was only a subtle awareness as silvery, violet-blue light, a scintillating Source-field in all directions to infinity. Then all light dissolved and disappeared, and I remained as pure Source awareness alone, the one without a second, the forever and ever bliss of freedom.

I remained absorbed in this state of pure Source consciousness for several hours, seven to be exact, before I contracted again into polarization and manifestation. When my body unlocked and my breathing returned to normal, I immediately noticed that the violet-blue light was still with me, bathing all in my vision with its scintillating radiance. I was fully anchored in the reality of Source, and wherever I looked, whatever I saw, was permeated with the light of unitive consciousness. I was firm in the conviction that I was Source and Source alone, a blissful ecstasy filling all and everything. I reclined and floated in the enlightening awareness as a reverberation from the core of my being continuously echoed: "I am free. . . . I am free. . . . I am Source. . . . I am one and free. . . ."

As I remained constant in Source awareness, the silence came to its appointed conclusion, and I was called to join Muktananda, who was in the United States. When I first saw him privately, he said to me, "You saw the cobra!" I nodded in the affirmative, too full of love to speak. He responded, "He does not show himself to everyone!" We wept together, and the constancy of our Sourceful love was palpable.

A short time later, Muktananda again advised me that I must have a period of integration and sent me away to a place where I could be quiet and away from the people who were always pursuing me. He also reminded me to remain secretive about my experiences. But my Source-field again attracted many people, and soon another illness forced me to remain quiet and in seclusion as much as possible.

After a year, I returned to join Muktananda for the conclusion of his American tour and his return to India. I served him as an ambassador with trips to Europe and other places where he himself could not go, and I assisted many in finding their way directly to him. Then I returned and joined him in India for the remaining months of his life.

Just before he died, Muktananda sent me off for another ambassadorial tour from India. As usual, before I left I saw him privately, and it was a remarkable meeting. He was sitting on his bed, and I sat facing him on the floor. We sat in silence for a long time, merging with each other in Source awareness. Then he spoke, saying, "Your destiny is with the masses. . . . You will find a way to share the eternal truth of one Source consciousness with the Western world. . . . You will know when to reveal your experience. . . . Your work will be great and go very well. . . . Always remember that I am with you in oneness. . . . I love you very much."

As he had done so many times before, he pulled me onto his lap and stroked my back, filling me to overflowing with bliss and love. Then, following another few moments of silence together, he dismissed me. I marveled at the strange completeness that I felt in our relationship. It was as if everything had been brought full circle. There was nothing left unsaid or undone between us.

Two days later, I arrived in New York, and when I arose after some rest I was informed that Muktananda, my beloved master, the beloved of hundreds of thousands, had died. I immediately returned to India for his death celebration and entombment. The death of an enlightening master is a time of celebration because it exemplifies an ultimate freedom beyond all form. It is the eternal liberation. Muktananda was buried traditionally within his ashram, according to all the scripturally prescribed rituals. Immediately after the ceremonies were concluded, I fell ill with another strange disease that demanded I remain secluded in bed for several weeks.

During these times, I was again elevated in silent equilibration and very expanded in subtle, multidimensional awareness. As I lay resting, the Divine Mother appeared in all her radiance. She anointed me and nurtured me like a mother tending her child, then covered me with flower petals. Then she said, "Now you must be independent. . . . You will always be with me. . . . Remember, I am always with you." Then she disappeared, and only her all-pervasive bliss remained, fully intoxicating the moment.

Soon thereafter, Muktananda appeared as I lay in seclusion. He was physical and three-dimensional, just as I had last seen him before he died. He anointed me and embraced me and then spoke, saying, "I have given you everything. . . . You are now Muktananda. . . . You are the bliss of freedom. . . . Remember, I am always with you—as you." He remained with me for a long time until we dissolved together into Sourceful awareness, and all that remained was the bliss of freedom.

Just as according to quantum mechanics as expressed by the new physics, there is a whole reality beyond the subatomic, so, too, beyond the quantum level there is an ultimate and unitive reality that is both immanent and transcendent and forever beyond. It is a pure awareness that is free and independent in its blissful oneness. To experience this reality is to be aware that you are but a wave within oceanic consciousness. Yet, just as the ocean is in a wave and a wave is in the ocean, so, too, Source is within you and you are within Source, a unity in diversity, an awareness free and unlimited unto forever.

The hours of my meditations have turned into days, and the days into years, and still the experience remains the same. Wherever I look, whatever I see, whatever I experience is Source and Source alone. There is no other, and as I peacefully witness this moment through the shimmering and scintillating blue haze of unitive awareness, I am aware that I am Source, that all is Source, that there is only one. I have become the bliss of freedom, and the whole of my being continually reverberates: I am one. . . . I am free. . . . I am all that is. . . . I am aware. . . . I am. . . . I . . .

EPILOGUE

What now
Unity delights in diversity
Radical entertainment
A theater of the absurd
I laugh
I cry
Here in the fullness of what is
And what is not
I watch
The forever-aware witness
Peaceful
Blissful
And full of love
I am
All is
One

Master Charles,
one year old.

Master Charles
with Santa Claus,
four years old.

Master Charles as a
five-year-old, sitting
on his front steps.

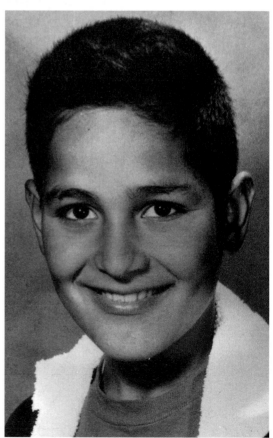

Master Charles
as a ten-year-old
schoolboy.

Master Charles (#64) as a high school senior
and captain of the football team.

Master Charles as a hippie
flower child at age twenty-one.

Photo of Muktananda that first awakened
Master Charles to his destiny (mentioned in Chapter 1).

"Remember—I'm Watching": Muktananda, 1970
(the photograph mentioned in Chapter 2).

Master Charles and Muktananda on front step, 1975
(the photograph mentioned in Chapter 7).

Master Charles as a young monk, 1977.

Master Charles with Muktananda, India, 1982.

Muktananda, 1979.

Synchronicity Conscious Living and Contemporary Meditation

To know Source is to be Source.
Meditate as Source.
Live as Source.
Master Charles

Here and now, in this moment, as I write these words across this page, I remain constant in awareness and firm in the conviction that I am — that all is — one Source consciousness, and that I am the eternal bliss of freedom. Wherever I look, I see the shimmering indigo blue play of unitive consciousness dancing and delighting as all and everything. Within this luminous energy field, millions of minute diamondlike particles of light scintillate and sparkle. Their eternal flux is spontaneous and creative, and the dance of each particle is an absolute abandon to ecstasy, the ecstasy of being one and free. All is enraptured with intoxicating bliss, the high of existence for the fun of it, for the sheer joy of being. This Sourceful inebriation saturates the whole of my multidimensional being with a lucid rapture that pleasures every cell of my physical body, and encompasses all forms, simultaneously radiating in all directions to infinity. All and everything is in love with itself, singing the one song, playing the one symphony, and reverberating the balanced harmonic of one Source celebrating itself for the sake of itself unto forever and ever.

I am also aware that there is but one equality consciousness, a unity in diversity, a delighting play for its own entertainment. I am aware that the symbols of Source that I manifested, the Divine Mother and Muktananda, are merely symbols within my particular database with regard to Source, God, deity, and truth. The ultimate truth is that Source is pure awareness; it is the one consciousness that is both manifest and unmanifest and forever beyond. All forms are but diversified awareness and ultimately dissolve into the eternal unity of pure, undifferentiated awareness.

Deity, God, reality—all are one Source consciousness, one equality consciousness, which is the essence of the whole of existence. Through all eyes, the one is looking. Through all hearts, the one is beating. Through all forms, the one is existing. Neither the manifest nor the unmanifest nor the forever beyond is anything other than Source. This unitive awareness is the bliss of freedom.

It is now 1996, and I have just entered my fifty-first year. Muktananda died in 1982, and it has been well over twenty years since I enjoyed many of the mystical experiences that I have shared in this book. Where am I now, and what is happening within the creative spontaneity of my journey? With love, I share the continuation.

When Muktananda was physically ill in the hospital, he told me that he was more than just a physical body and that within the multidimensional awareness of Source he was eternally blissful. He also said, "Physical death comes sooner or later—what difference does it make? It's just a changing of clothes within the diversity of Source awareness. . . . If not now—in five years." He said this to me in 1977, and he left his body exactly five years later, in 1982. Anchored within the purity of Source awareness, he was omniscient, for this field contains all information.

Muktananda also told me that I would write this book and not to reveal my mystical experiences until I did. He told me to find a way to contemporize the ancient and eternal truth of one Source consciousness, and the art of meditation, and share it within my culture and the Western world. I have endeavored to fulfill his wishes.

Following Muktananda's death, I completed my work with the formal organization that I and many had built with him. We had generated a multimillion-dollar empire across the world, yet I left with only a few dollars in my pocket—money that he had given me and told me never to spend. I still have it today. I returned to the United States, for I am an American, and settled in the Blue Ridge Mountains of Virginia. My only intention was to live my freedom, to enjoy my Source awareness, and to share it with whomever was interested. I wanted to remain alone and quiet for a while, away from the public, to just be in the fullness of my blissful state of being.

I relinquished my shaven head and saffron robes, grew my hair out, and returned to appropriate Western dress for a monk. I Westernized my name, becoming Brother Charles, Charles being my given name and Brother to include my monkhood and the equality of consciousness, brothers and sisters in the one, which is my experience. I stayed in a small house within a sylvan environment thirty miles from the nearest town. I lived my bliss and continued within the celebration of my freedom.

One day many years ago, Muktananda had said to me, "You are like me—you have the boon of attracting people." He was referring to the state of enlightening reverberation that naturally entrains everyone and everything to it like a magnet. This is just what happens within the energetic frequency dynamics of oneness. Before I knew it, a few people found me in my simple hermitage and asked if they could be with me. From five it became ten, from ten twenty, and so on, until now I am surrounded by a whole community of loving people. This community assists me in meeting the demands of ever-increasing numbers of people who want to participate in my sharing. The members of this community have dedicated their lives to meditation and conscious living, and they journey it on a daily basis.

An organization has been created, the Synchronicity Foundation, and a Sanctuary with facilities for retreats not far from the simple house in which I first settled when I arrived here in Virginia. Now, a steady stream of meditators find their way to this rustic hermitage from all over the world. I have become a Muktananda for them, as I share the truth as I experience it and guide them within their own meditative unfolding. I love them as I love myself, and I delight in their ever-expanding awareness. This is my continuing fulfillment. For is it not the destiny of a flower to be enjoyed for its beauty and fragrance, and for the truthful exemplification that it embodies? I am blissful within the continuing celebration of life.

A few years ago, some people said that their experience of me was as a master of meditation and suggested that my name be changed to Master Charles. I assumed this name not merely because of what I know about the mystical meditative journey and my fifty years of experience, but more important, because of what I am — the constant reverberation of Sourceful freedom. The free set others free; it is inevitable. I watch within the blissful delight of this entertaining journey of unitive existence. It is as it is. It is appropriate.

Muktananda had asked me to contemporize the ancient and time-honored truth of meditation and Source awareness, and to share it with the Western world in a context that is more easily understandable and acceptable. I began this work while he was still alive, and I have continued unto this present time. It has become known as Synchronicity, the Art and Science of Conscious Living, a New Empirical Mysticism. Synchronicity Contemporary Meditation and Synchronicity High-Tech Meditation, the Neurotechnology of Bliss, have become trademarks for this contemporary Western form of meditation, and many thousands of people have been assisted in experiencing meditation as a result. It continues to expand with every passing day.

Synchronicity, the New Empirical Mysticism, reflects the context of the emerging spirituality of our times. It combines science and mysticism to validate the ancient truth of one Source consciousness. The ancient art of meditation has now become the art and science of meditation. Source in its macrocosmic aspect can now be easily understood through the new science paradigm at the cutting edge of quantum mechanics, which proves there is but one reality that expresses itself as a unity in diversity. In its microcosmic aspect, this can be related scientifically to the polarization of opposites, duality and nonduality, as exemplified within the human brain. Simply stated, when the two hemispheres of the brain are imbalanced in function, there is duality and limited awareness. When the hemispheres are balanced, or synchronized, there is nonduality and unlimited awareness. As is easy to see, the truth is eternal, but the ways of understanding it change constantly.

When meditation is studied within this scientific paradigm, it is revealed as a synchronizing experience within the brain. This process decelerates the brain waves and proportionately increases whole-brain synchronicity. Since the brain is the control center for the human body, when synchronized and whole in its function, the experience within the body is radically different. Not only is the state of experience termed metanormal, or nonordinary, but it includes the full gamut of what the ancients termed *enlightened experience*. Interestingly, meditation catalyzes the increased production of neurochemicals such as endorphins, which are the natural opiates within the human biochemistry. The meditative state of whole-brain synchrony is associated with intoxicating opiates, and when it becomes constant, one is consistently inebriated within a nondual awareness of reality. This is a contemporary demonstration of the bliss of freedom. Since brain function can be patterned and constancy developed, regular meditation is now validated in its capacity to unfold the optimum in whole-brain synchronization, or the metanormal state of human experience known in the ancient systems as enlightenment. A Muktananda, then, or any enlightening master, is merely one who has become constant in the state of whole-brain synchrony. Since technology flows inherently out of the scientific paradigm, Western culture has excelled in its development. One pertinent example is the precision that has been brought to the technology of sound. The effect of sound on the brain has been studied in depth, and when applied to meditation, opens windows of opportunity as never before. Since ancient meditators had to retire to caves for isolation and purity of vibrational space, would it not be appropriate if we could bring a contemporary "cave" to everyone's brain through precision-sound technology? Then meditation would be easily available for anyone, with or without a cave. Considering life in the modern Western world, this is essential, for how many caves are there in relation to the total population? Therefore, thanks to the ever-expanding diversification of unity, we now have precision technological meditation. How does it work?

Certain patterns in sound can entrain the brain into hemispheric synchronization. When conveyed through the isolation of stereophonic headphones, meditation becomes a precision experience of entrainment. Now it becomes High-Tech Meditation, which is exactly what I meant when I coined those words fourteen years ago. I contemporized meditation by creating a sound technology that can be combined with other sounds, such as music or the sounds of nature, a technology that enhances the deceleration of brain waves and increases whole-brain synchrony. When listened to through stereophonic headphones, it delivers precision meditation. The cave has now come to our ears. This is the Neurotechnology of Bliss.

Because sound is a vibrational energetic and can be conveyed through an electromagnetic medium, Synchronicity Contemporary Meditation can be shared through the audiotape-recorded format. It is made available in correspondence course and program formats that facilitate meditation on a daily basis no matter what a person's lifestyle. All that is required is a cassette tape player and a set of stereo headphones. Statistics from research on contemporary meditators from all walks of life using Synchronicity technology over the last twelve years validate that it is a precision meditation experience that can deliver the benefits of long-term meditation in a fraction of the time. Yet, the enduring proof is the equilibrated experience of many thousands of people who have radically expanded their awareness and consistently enjoy the benefits of unitive consciousness: true freedom, pure creativity, peace, and bliss.

All participating in the Synchronicity Contemporary Meditation experience are supported through modern telecommunications. From our headquarters at the Synchronicity Sanctuary, they regularly receive guidance on their meditative journey via telephone communication no matter where they are in the world. The assistance of the mystical master of meditation is globally available as never before for those who take advantage of it. What an incredible journey for the contemporary mystic—the miracle of the ever-creative diversifications of one unity!

There are also Synchronicity Contemporary Meditation retreats and programs for those who wish to directly experience what I am. Whether I am in residence at the Synchronicity Sanctuary or traveling in other parts of the world, I am always available in such contexts to share my experience with whomever is interested. In this way, I continue to facilitate many thousands of people within the intricacies of the meditative art and science.

Since it is the nature of reality in phenomenal manifestation to expand, the world of Synchronicity Contemporary Meditation is continually unfolding. From this simple and rustic hermitage here in the Blue Ridge Mountains of Virginia, it grows internationally, as through it people experience the truth at the core of their own being: the enlightening truth of one Source as all and everything, the enlightening experience of the bliss of freedom.

As for me, I remain ecstatic as I fulfill the wishes of my beloved master to share the truth through meditation in a contemporary Western way. Many come to drink at this well, and it is always overflowing because it is not mine to control or possess in any limiting way. Rather, I am just a hollow bamboo through which flows the Sourceful totality of what is. It flows unencumbered because I remain a forever-aware witness merged within the intoxicating bliss of the one without a second.

My continuing vision for these times in which we find ourselves manifest remains anchored in Sourceful awareness. There is but one equality consciousness, a unity in diversity, and we are truly one and free. Every day, more and more people awaken to this truth within themselves and expand their awareness of who they really are. Whereas people used to believe that they were merely human beings with occasional experiences of Source, they are now becoming aware that they are Sourceful beings exploring being human. It is after all but a Creation Game for the fun of it,

for the sheer joy of the playing. And as individual awareness expands, there are simultaneous and proportional
shifts within collective awareness. This is particularly evidenced in the West.

The mystical as a collective experience has been largely
absent within Western spirituality. Many have been seeking it unconsciously based on the awareness of its absence.
It is not that there is anything wrong. Rather, it has been
an idea whose time had not yet come. The Western form
was evolving within the play of consciousness. Now, however, it is soon to become manifest and bring itself to its
flowering. It finds its emergent roots within the new scientific mysticism and the neurotechnologies of bliss. It can
no longer be found in stale religions that have reduced the
truly spiritual to mere social clubs mired in the perpetuation of limited, ego-level dualistic dogmas and stuck in the
repetitive performance of unconscious rituals. It will rather
be found as countless human beings burst beyond ego,
journey to the center of their beings, and consciously manifest their unconscious and insatiable spiritual yearnings
as the mystical awareness of truthful oneness.

The contemporary paradigm of this Western emergence
is an empirical mysticism. Whereas we used to confine
our worship to churches and temples, we now begin to
recognize, through meditative expansion of awareness, that
the most sacred place of worship is within our own hearts,
at the very center of our being. For therein we discover
that deity, the ultimate Source of all that is, is our very own
consciousness. Once we experience it within ourselves, we
simultaneously experience it as everyone and everything.
Then, within the truthful awareness of one equality consciousness, we easily relinquish our limited beliefs and our

relentless imposition of them upon one another. We no longer fight and kill because of natural diversities such as race, religion, and political systems. Rather, we truthfully recognize that every time we hate, murder, or impose our limitations upon a seeming other, we violate the God that we say we honor. For all allegiance to any God, whatever name we use, is useless and fraudulent when we violate and dishonor the God that is manifest as ourselves and as every human being, verily, the one Source that is all and everything and forever beyond. This awareness embodies true mystical expression. It delivers everyone to the bliss of freedom.

This is the way that we bring about the mastery of being human and fulfill our primary responsibility to experience Source through the human form. We demonstrate that awareness is not a commodity. It cannot be possessed. It cannot be made another object to ourselves as a subject. Pure awareness is nondual and forever beyond all polarity. Only when we meditate to simply be as we are, aware—not to gain some thing or attain some goal, or to get anywhere we are not already—do we reveal to ourselves, through a pure intention that yields ego transcendence, the pure awareness that is the ultimate reality. Then, as Source awareness, we simply live within the equality of one consciousness, a unity within diversity.

This then is my vision: ever-increasing numbers of conscious human beings expressing the truthful awareness of the one Source that eternally celebrates itself as all and everything. Such celebration is the only authentic ritual. It is conscious living. It is the forever-delighting enjoyment of true freedom. Meditation is the means, as through its equilibrating window we return ourselves to wholeness once again. Then life is blissful, peaceful, and full of love.

In conclusion, I leave you with a story that I often tell. Once there was a man who wanted to know the difference between heaven and hell. He contemplated this question in detail but could not figure it out. When he was thoroughly confused, the Lord compassionately appeared and said, "Come, I'll show you." The Lord took the man to a hotel with many identical rooms. Entering the first room, he noticed a group of people sitting around a large bowl of soup. The soup was deliciously fragrant, yet all the people were emaciated and starving. They were negative and miserably abusive to one another. At first the man could not understand, but then he noticed that they all had spoons twice as long as their arms. When they tried to get the soup into their mouths, they missed. Their suffering was indeed intense, and the Lord said, "This is hell. Come, I'll show you heaven." The Lord took the man to an identical room across the hall. In this room was the same bowl of deliciously fragrant soup. But the group surrounding it were full-bellied and blissful. Love was palpable, and everyone was celebrating joyously. Suddenly, the man became perplexed, for he noticed that they, too, had the same spoons with handles twice as long as their arms. When the man reached the peak of his confusion, the Lord interrupted him, saying, "This is heaven, because they have learned to feed one another."

Transformation in the individual is simultaneously transformation in the universal. When we first recognize the truth within ourselves, then it is inevitable that we also recognize it in one another. The way out is in, and it delivers us all to the bliss of freedom.

Finally, I have shared my experience within this book. I am not asking that you blindly believe all that I have described here. Rather, through the consideration of it, I hope that you will explore the same experience within yourself. For, truly, I am a human being just like you, and what is potential within me is also potential within you and every human being. If you search within yourself, I am sure you will experience what I and many like me have experienced. Beyond the mind, forever beyond all interpretations, the ultimate truth is always available. It awaits you at the center of your own being. It offers no less than your very freedom, and true freedom is always blissful.

Therefore, meditate, meditate, meditate. . . .

As far as I am concerned, just as the world is as you see it based on your interpretations, so also I am as you see me. Yet, if through the meditative expansion of awareness, you move beyond your mind and its illusory limitations, you will see me as I see myself. And what is that? It is as it is, for, very truthfully, I see myself as I am.

I acknowledge you in the awareness of our oneness. I wish you love and peace. I wish you the bliss of freedom.

To Find Out More About Synchronicity
Conscious Living and Contemporary Meditation

Originated in 1983 by Master Charles, Synchronicity Foundation is a nonsectarian, not-for-profit organization dedicated to the conscious exploration of the Sourceful human experience through the technological approach to the art and science of meditation known as Synchronicity Contemporary High-Tech Meditation. In addition to having distributed over a million Contemporary High-Tech Meditation tapes, Synchronicity offers regular Conscious Living and Contemporary Meditation programs and retreats with Master Charles in an international network of Synchronicity Centers in the United States, Europe, and Australia.

For more information about our meditation tapes, our correspondence program, and retreats with Master Charles, visit our Internet website at http://www.synchronicity.org or contact:

Synchronicity Foundation
P.O. Box 694
Nellysford, VA 22958
(804) 361-2323
Orders: 1-800-962-2033